SORRY YOU'RE NOT HERE

Askew's Word on the Lake Anthology 2020

Fiction, Nonfiction, and Poetry from **Contest Winners** and **Presenters**

Design and typography by (studio)Effigy

Edited by Scott Fitzgerald Gray

The Word on the Lake Writers' Festival is a nonprofit celebration of the written word, organized and presented annually by the Shuswap Association of Writers. All sales of the *Askew's Word on the Lake Anthology 2020* go directly toward supporting Word on the Lake.

Table of Contents

From the Shuswap Association of Writers

This is a somewhat bittersweet prelude, insofar as it introduces the first expanded edition of the *Word on the Lake Anthology* — featuring not only the winners of the seventh annual Askew's Word on the Lake Writing Contest, but also a selection of writings from some of the presenters at the 2020 Word on the Lake Writers' Festival.

Except there will be no Word on the Lake this year.

Like so many other gatherings, conferences, and public events, Word on the Lake has been cancelled for 2020 because of the spread of the suitably sinisterly named SARS-CoV-2 coronavirus. The title for this year's anthology, taken from the poem "Me and the Pigeon in Tuscany," was chosen as an ironic nod to this development, represented by people across the world holding fast where they are to protect the health and lives of those around them.

The decision to cancel the festival for the first time in seventeen years was a heartbreaking one — but also an easy one, insofar as the readers, writers, presenters, and volunteers who come together to create Word on the Lake are Word on the Lake. There's no festival without the people who make it happen, and that fact makes all those people worth protecting.

At the time I write this, things in British Columbia and beyond are still uncertain. But one thing we all know — as readers, as writers — is that in times like these, everyone needs stories.

In this book, the contest winners and presenters of the 2020 Word on the Lake Writer's Festival-that-might-have-been are proud to share some of our stories.

Thanks to all those who submitted to the Askew's Word on the Lake Writing Contest, for your dedication to writing and your continuing support of Word on the Lake.

Thanks to all the presenters who have graciously allowed us to present their work herein.

Thanks to Mary-Lou McCausland and Virginia McCausland, for starting up and shepherding the writing contest and the *Word on the Lake Anthology*.

Thanks to Askew's for their continued support of the writing contest, the anthology, Word on the Lake, and the arts in Salmon Arm.

Wherever you are right now, thank you for being here with us as well.

— Scott Fitzgerald Gray
for the board and members of
the Shuswap Association of Writers

From Our **Contest Sponsor**
Askew's

My grandfather, R.B. (Dick) Askew, arrived in Salmon Arm in 1919, just after the 1918 flu pandemic. At the time, it might have been difficult to envision a recovery. But as we see from history, people are resilient, and we will rebound from the current COVID-19 crisis.

One hundred years after Dick Askew's humble beginning as manager of the EA Palmer and Co. meat market, we at Askew's, the company he founded in 1929, are focused on the people whose lives have been impacted by the virus: our customers, employees, and the community at large. Askew's stores are all working hard to serve our loyal customers in Salmon Arm, Armstrong, and Sicamous. We are a family business and are very proud of all of the dedicated people who work at Askew's and who are helping serve our communities.

Art provides comfort, wisdom, resilience, and the means for self-expression and connection. As the world grapples with the unprecedented and difficult challenges posed by COVID-19, the importance of all that art provides is even more significant. Hence, we are pleased to continue to support the Askew's Word on the Lake Writing Contest and the writers who participate.

— David Askew
President, Askew's

Askew's
Quality & Service Since 1929

"There is so much to read and the days are so short! I get more hungry for knowledge every day, and less able to satisfy my hunger."

— Mary Ann Evans (George Eliot)

PONDERINGS

S. MAGGIE RICCIARDI

Are phobias hereditary?
Occurring and mutating down the years
Like unwanted guests who will not leave?
Why do we fear falls from high places?
Were we chased up high cliffs by bullying soldiers?
Cast from a ship's crow's nest in a violent storm?
Perhaps after eons in the canopy,
Walking upright was hard to learn?

Did claustrophobia mark the miner,
Working, and often dying for his family,
His very livelihood at stake?
Agoraphobia? Standing on platforms,
Above the crowd, in blazing sun,
Publicly shamed and humiliated
As rough fingers probed
Our naked black skin?

Arachnophobia? What Victorian child
Would not have it? Locked away
In a cobwebbed closet for some minor misdemeanour?

Throw fear of the dark in with that one.
Did some long-ago explorer's first encounter with an anaconda
Result in us screaming at a garter snake?
Has the threat of throwing them to the sharks been
Passed from convict ancestors to me?

We talk of talents, 'the musical one'
Maybe his Italian grandmother or Welsh grandfather
Called and sang across ancient reverberating valleys.
That Olympic runner inherited his athleticism from
Forbears running barefoot between African villages.
A Parisian courtesan, seeking to please, handed down
Her sense of style to a teenage descendant in Montreal?

But who can account for the geniuses?
Rare, seemingly random, occasionally 'crazy' beyond belief.
Who can explain them, and who would want to?
No doubt scientists will unravel these genetic mysteries.
Meanwhile we can ponder and marvel. It is enough
To know they continue to exist.

HONOURABLE MENTION — **POETRY**

"Ponderings" is about genetic memory and the beautiful mutation that is genius. Eschewing overt didacticism, which can be a turn-off in poetry, the writer articulates queries based on observation and leaves the answers to us. Responding to the most important questions — how do we connect in our "cobwebbed closets"? — they give us the reassurance of a canon that returns to its source: harmony.

— Linda Rogers

Sold

RICHARD KELLY KEMICK

My father is a cabinetmaker. As such, my brother, Tress, and I spent a large part of our childhood at job sites, in the weird world of other people's houses. During these outings, Tress and I were to remain quiet and nearby, pacing the room for dropped screws. British sentries have a similar job description but work a mere two hours before getting four off. Tress and I were afforded no such luxury, because the only time my father took a break was to sleep at night, something I imagined he did ramrod straight, arms across his chest.

One time at a job site, he was sanding the underside of a kitchen counter and gashed his forehead but refused to pause. When the customer came into the kitchen, my father emerged; his entire forehead had flowered with blood. "Oh my god," the customer said.

"What?" my father replied, oblivious, as he wiped the back of his hand across his brow, an action which made the overall effect — and I can't stress this enough — much, much worse.

My father approaches woodworking the same way he did parenting: as something perfected in Gothic Europe that was now deviated from only for reasons of new-age laziness: an unrelenting exactness, a conflation of rigour and morality, and a deep-seated suspicion of daydreaming — or, as he called it, "sitting there with a thumb up your ass."

In fact, the only act of imagination he enjoyed was that first moment someone saw their new cabinets. As blood flowed down my father's face, the customer's attention was pulled to imagining the life that the renovated kitchen promised. These moments were always the same: hands traced along the countertop's corners, the eyeballed appreciation of the cupboard doors, that first pull on a cutlery drawer which extended so smooth and deep that the action was repeated, again and again, in an unwittingly sexual manner.

Who knows if that customer still lives there? That house could've changed hands six or eight times by now. I can tell you, however, that those kitchen cabinets still stand immaculate. I know this because my father made the cabinetry in the Kemick house, woodwork which will outlive us all.

The Kemick house, after thirty years of ownership, is up for sale. Well, kind of. It's up for rent. But that's just to squeeze out a bit of cash as my parents gallivant around the globe like landed gentry. The crawlspace has been boxed up and donated; the office, scanned and shredded; the memory chest, unpacked and recycled. This renting idea is only temporary. Once that dries up, they'll sell it. The writing, as they say, is on the wall.

Not these specific walls, mind you. God, no. As teenagers, Tress and I were not even allowed to *touch* the walls, lest we smudge up the paint with our pubescent greases; and if our father caught us, either in the act or through forensic evidence, we would be forced to walk down our driveway, across the sidewalk, and to the street, which we were to then touch with our hand, all the while our father's silhouette watched from behind the French drapes to ensure our fingertips came into physical contact with the asphalt. The idea, I think, was to inconvenience us into obedience.

Growing up, I was always jealous of my friends. Their fathers seemed so relaxed, so hip, so laissez-faire about the thermostat. They had trendy jobs in departments like 'acquisitions' or 'communications,' workplaces where it was assumedly uncouth to gush blood across the new countertop. And because of these jobs, their families were always moving — not so often cities but houses, into ones bigger, better, ever farther into Calgary's orbital suburbs.

These were the years I would lie on our living room's carpet and watch reruns of *Friends*, as my whole body ached with how far Calgary-South was from where I wanted to be. From our split-level at the end of the C-train line, I didn't even know where the closest café with upholstered furniture was.

"Come help me fix the hot water tank," my father interrupted, turning off the television. "You have to the count of one," he added, and then, without pause, said, "One."

I rose with tortured angst. "I cannot wait," I said, "to have a landlord."

How was I to know that there would come a day when I would be desperate for the house, ravenous for every scrap of its memory: every birthday card, every screaming match, every washing machine buzzer, every commercial break; the light through the Venetian blinds, the smell of Windex, the mosquito-like whine of the table saw from the garage? Who will remember what we loved?

I no longer pray to God, but I did when I lived in the house. Back then, I conceived of a god who was constant yet itinerant, one who roamed the Earth like a hitchhiker, who watched sunsets from treetops, who heard our pleas through Discman headphones. Someone who planned our futures, righted all wrongs, and showed us that nothing was ever truly lost.

Now, if forced to articulate it, the god I believe in seems a lot like the Kemick house: something inanimate and immovable, one that envelopes all reality, and that you move through like blood within a heart; something that's hard to believe existed before your life began and impossible to imagine no longer existing while you continue to. And isn't it possible or even probable, isn't it a law of thermodynamics, that since energy cannot be destroyed but needs somewhere to go, that all of the astonishment, envy, glee, sorrow, rage, shame, and exultation—all of it has seeped into the woodwork and drywall, and after years upon years, a kind of sentience has formed? And that sentience is what's being sold, a thought which — now that I think about it — only proves my metaphor more.

I moved out at 17, my brother having left the year before. There's only so long a person can tolerate being micromanaged on how to unload a dishwasher before the suitcase packs itself. With Tress and me gone, thus commenced 'the decade of renovations.' These renovations, however, were different from the renovations of my youth. *Those* renovations were about making the house ours, such as when my father ripped out every bathroom vanity to replace them with ones twenty centimetres taller, since our family all have the body shape of uncooked fettuccine. *These* new renovations, however, aren't borne of making the house ours but of making the house anyone's; *these* renovations are characterized by beige baseboards, dimmer switches on every light, and prying free the faux-wood paneling. *These* renovations give the scent of a hotel, each room absent any whiff of artistic offence.

During this time, when I visited, I'd have these daydreams of writing letters to the house's future families, telling them the truth of where they live: why the bathroom vanities are so tall, where in the backyard the guinea pig is buried, how I'm sure that there is still — after all these years — clumps of dog hair in the bowels of the central vac and, upon discovery, these should be treated like a relic from a saint. I planned to time-capsule these letters in the dead centre of the living room floor before the hardwood was laid overtop, but every time I started to write, I'd turn inept to the point of illiterate. My pen hovered above the paper and everything I wanted to say turned to silt, crashing around me for an ungraspable moment before being pulled out to sea. Because isn't that another law of thermodynamics, something about entropy, something about all of existence in a slow state of ebb, the universe expanding while we stay static? How to convey what your life meant to you?

We aren't even the house's original owners: a fact I'd always known but hadn't really understood, the way you know your partner dated people before you but don't really understand the significance until the two of you run into that person at Costco and their shopping cart has *significantly* better items.

I was in grade nine, and one evening, we ventured into the dining room (a room which, until I was far too old to now admit, I thought was called the *dying* room, in opposition, of course, to the *living* room). My father unhung the painting of the Ontario winter scene, Tress closed the curtains, and I cleared the table, where my mother set up a Kodak Carousel projector. She was showing us slides of when she'd backpacked Australia.

The cone of light spread against the wall, and my mother narrated her way through each photo, slipping gradually but pervasively into the accent. Each slide sounded its thud and grind as we rotated through the koalas and farmsteads and an ocean that never ends. But then a surprise, one that shocked the Australian accent right out of my mother. Across our wall, shone two strangers on their wedding day.

"Those are the previous owners," my mother said. "That crawlspace is so messy, their pictures must've mixed up with ours."

"Previous owners of what?" I asked, but my mother didn't answer. She continued to flip through the slides—the wedding reception, the honeymoon, and then the house. Our house. Hand-held before the front door. And it felt as if we had stumbled upon a picture of a ghost. The air grew cold with an otherworldly presence, as all around us—in the dying room—the drywall darkened and stood like tombstones, holding knowledge of a world we would never know.

The best memory I have of the house is not something that happened but something that didn't:

Christmas Eve '95, making my brother seven and me almost six. Our parents were in the kitchen as Tress and I got ready for bed upstairs. PJs on, our bodies quivered with anticipation.

In the days leading to Christmas, I would sometimes turn so overwrought with excitement that I would scream, shrill and sudden, like a pressure cooker with a leaky gasket. And while my mother was bemused by these vibratos, my father insisted that they were the cause of his worsening deafness and not the decades of working with power tools without ear protection.

While my brother and I rinsed our toothbrushes, I let slip a scream, and my father charged up the stairs. "I saw Santa!" he said. "Through the kitchen window."

My heart fell right into my rectum.

Our kitchen window faces west, as does my parents' bedroom window, to which the three of us sprinted to stare at the sky of our suburb, through the soft grey of light pollution.

"He was heading over Bob and Bonnie's," my father said, and we craned our necks southwards. My palms suctioned against the glass as I searched — frantic — for the sleigh. But we did not see it.

A sparse snow began to fall, and the thought that my father's sighting was but a trick — a life lesson in the pitfalls of credulity — slowly took hold of me, and my palms unpuckered from the window. But then, as my father continued to scrutinize the skyline, he said, under his breath, "For fuck's sake." And for the fact that he swore, and that he did so only to himself, the way he does when installing a cabinet, showed that he truly was searching, that he, too, believed, and my heart, which had elevatored its way out of my colon, began to grow, swelling throughout my entire chest.

You inevitably become one of the things you surround yourself with. Over time, even the hardest membranes soak into something permeable, and the sentience of the woodwork and drywall bleeds back into you. I think that, also, is a law of science: osmosis. But is there a name for the opposite, of things separating at the seams, of putting a section of yourself up for sale? Google says it is called, simply, reverse osmosis, but there must be a term unto itself, something obscure and unpronounceable, something grade twelve students spend hours memorizing only to forget immediately after the final when they retreat to the convenience store parking lot, smoke American cigarettes, drink pineapple liqueur, and glow with immortality; life before the migration, before moving apartments every eighteen months, before mass-made cabinetry; before identity becomes a process not of addition but subtraction.

Who will remember what we loved? No one. That's the point. That is the impetus that demands we love: an act of such servitude we'd never do it otherwise.

What makes the Santa memory the best memory is not an appraisal of its joy but its clarity. Even now, just to think of it still summons an intoxication: my lungs unable to inflate, my scalp at atingle, my mind reeling like water sloshed in a basin; the feeling that something of tremendous importance and beauty, of unsurpassable rarity, something of soul-changing significance was on the cusp of arrival. For we, surely, were at the landmark of our lives, our futures built of pure potential, nothing but promise, all within our very own home.

A SYMPHONY OF SPARROWS

SHARON MCINNES

Through the crowd of Christmas shoppers, I see you, near the escalator, leaning on a post. As if you're waiting for someone. The bustle, the noise, the unfamiliar faces, they disappear. You turn your head, look at me. As if you knew.

Now you're walking toward me, squinting. "Barbara?"

My intention is to smile nonchalantly. I'm not sure what my face actually does. "Hi, Luke."

"Wow — good to see you!"

"Same." Your hair is still the color of straw. Shorter though, and thinner. My father called you "Sheep Dog" way back then. Pissed me right off. Until you, I was an obedient daughter.

"I heard you're living in the Kootenays."

"Yep." You need a shave. Unless this is a new style?

"You here for Christmas, to see your folks?"

"Mom. Dad died six months ago."

You touch my arm and grimace. "I'm sorry."

I nod again. "Lung cancer." Dad said you weren't my type; you were doomed to fail. Well, you did fail that one attempt, jumping from East Bridge. Did you really want to die?

Your eyes are filled with compassion. They seem greener than they used to be.

Now I remember the poems you sent me when you ran away. Your mother called it that, "running away," even though you were seventeen, almost an adult. And the poems? So much feeling, but bad spelling and punctuation. But hey, look at bill bissett. Maybe you were trying to emulate him?

"I'm sorry we lost touch." You do look sorry, or guilty, maybe. Although it wasn't your fault. I was the one who got married.

"Me too." Now I remember the last time I saw you, at the Safeway on Fourth, a week before the wedding. You wished me a happy life. Walking home, I was overcome with the urge to call off the wedding. I told Mom I wasn't sure anymore. She said that was common, it was just cold feet, I'd get over it, be happy. Plus, the invitations were sent out, the presents bought.

"Say, you want to take a break, grab a coffee, catch up?"

Something furious rushes through my veins. *No. No, I have to get back to Mom's. No, I can't.* These are my thoughts. I say, "Okay."

We ride the long escalator up toward natural light. Memories surface. Long drives in your yellow Chevy, Mick Jagger in the background. *Time is on my side.* I liked how the word *time* got stretched way out, like time sometimes does, like it did those afternoons. You drove with one arm slipped through the steering wheel, your fingers tapping the dashboard, your other arm draped over my shoulder. I had to slouch in the seat. A seventeen-year-old, it turns out, *can* know what love is, even though my mother called it infatuation. From "fatuous," inanely foolish. She was wrong about that but right about my getting hurt. *You deserve someone smart and ambitious*—those were the words on the note you left in my coat pocket. You had it wrong too.

We walk along Granville. I carry a red umbrella; you duck under it. It's cold up here but not cold enough to turn the rain to snow. Were we together in the winter? I remember warm summer days. Afternoons lying on sand dunes, our fingers entwined, telling stories. Today our footsteps on the sidewalk keep time.

I need to do something, now, to save myself. I turn to you. "So, how's Kate?" The day I saw your wedding photo in the local paper, a vise had gripped my heart and squeezed.

"It didn't work out."

"No?"

"No. It was my fault. I was an asshole." (I can believe this.) "What about you? Are you married?"

"Yes." Michael's smart. And ambitious. He works for the town but has big plans. I don't say he plays golf on weekends and doesn't care for rock and roll. I don't say he's a good man, or we're trying to have a child, or he's at Mom's right now doing a bunch of jobs around the house. Just, "Yes."

The only table left in the SkyTrain station coffee shop is small and needs wiping. I go get a napkin, do a half-assed job of making it presentable. I am stalling, afraid. So I try to lighten the mood, my mood. "Do you remember the time we took my little sister to English Bay?"

You laugh. "I do!"

"You slid down the water slide holding a bottle of beer in the air. She loved that."

"I remember."

Under the table our knees touch. I don't move mine away. Neither do you. I'm scared. We order coffees and share a huge piece of carrot cake with cream-cheese icing. I do not normally eat sweets of any kind. We talk about the past, which, according to my yoga teacher, does not exist. *Only this moment is real:* that's her mantra. In this moment, I have a longing to feel your skin on mine. Even your hand in mine would work. This thought triggers a knot in my centre, and I begin to unravel, slowly, one loose thread at a time.

You tell me you live in the West End. I've always wanted to live there, on the edge of Stanley Park, overlooking the harbor. It's been a lifelong fantasy. The West End is a world away from Kaslo. I do like home, though — the quiet, the peace, the friendliness. I should tell you that. Instead I hear myself say: "What's your place like?"

"I lucked out, got into a great old house on Barclay. I have the upper floor."

There's a pause. We sip our coffees. You tilt your head. "Would you like to see it?" You ask the question innocently, as if you're some hip, laid-back realtor offering to show a client a new listing, no pressure, whatever.

This is the moment. I can save myself right now. I am a faithful wife, a school teacher for God's sake; we're trying to have a baby; Michael loves me. I couldn't live with myself if I cheated. These thoughts flash in my thirty-four-year-old brain with the insistence of a strobe light.

I say, "Sure." But it's a lie. No part of me is sure. Most of me is hollering *NO!!* The part that says yes is new — or maybe old. But I can still save myself, later. Maybe you have no intention of trying to seduce me. That was never your style.

The house is a restored mansion, grey-green and white. In front, a massive weeping willow full of noisy house sparrows, even now in winter, takes up most of the yard. The birds chatter madly: *What are you doing? Have you lost your mind?* The path you and I take is made of circular stepping stones encircled by moss.

When we walk in, I see myself in the tall mahogany-framed mirror in the foyer. I see dark hair, in a bob, and the blue woolen scarf that Michael gave me last Christmas wrapped around a neck, but I don't recognize myself. You lead me up, up a long flight of stairs. I am aware of the curve of your buttocks in your jeans. They're worn, not fake-worn but for real. You open the door, which is unlocked. This seems risky to me.

Inside, you take my coat, place my shopping bags tenderly on the floor near the door. What was I expecting? Not this, not cleanliness and order, not exquisite old furniture, not framed art on the walls. You look at me. "Do you still drink CC?"

"I do. With Diet Coke."

You smile. "Some things never change, eh?"

"I guess." This is no time to argue. I wander around the living room looking at the paintings. I'm trying to distract myself. Or maybe giving myself time to come to my senses. You tell me the paintings belonged to your grandmother. I remember her from a Thanksgiving dinner at your parents' place. I can still hear her raucous laughter, see her thick white hair pulled off her face with silver barrettes. You say she died two years ago. "She had a good life though."

A good life? Did she? How could you tell?

Do I?

We talk. I find myself laughing. Way too much. But it feels so good. You are a great storyteller. I wonder if your grammar has improved too?

Twenty-seven minutes later, I am running my hand across flannelette sheets decorated with exotic birds — toucans and macaws and motmots. Now I am watching you slip your soft black T-shirt over your head. Your shoulders are wider now, and stronger. You wait. I reach for you. The past takes the present in its arms. Outside the window, I hear the house sparrows singing like crazy, a veritable symphony. I have no idea what they're trying to say.

Second Place — **Fiction**

I felt that the author's portrayal of the characters in this piece, and especially the conflicting emotions in the central character were very strong. I felt pulled into the story (which should always be the writer's intention), and particularly drawn to the narrator's struggles with right and wrong even as the reader knows how this is going to go. I was also very impressed with the on-the-nose and very believable dialogue.

— David A. Poulsen

In **Search** of the **Red-Winged Blackbird**

Sally Quon

When the stress of the day becomes too much for me, and I need a moment to collect myself, I retreat to the cool darkness of my basement bedroom. I turn the computer screen towards the bed and put on a slide show of the pictures I've taken over the last few months. The one I've chosen today is called "Reflections", and it's all about water — marshes and ponds, mountain streams, rivers and lakes.

The pictures soothe me. I was there. I saw that. I can feel the stress leaving my body and my mind becomes clear. Things are not as overwhelming as they seemed. The obstacles are not so high. I can get through this.

The camera was a Mother's Day present from my husband and children. I cried when I opened it. I didn't deserve a gift like that. My husband and I had recently separated and my kids were in foster care. What kind of a mother did that make me? I had wished for the whole day to just pass by, unacknowledged, but special occasions don't go away because you want them to. Not when you have kids.

It was a couple of months before I even opened the box.

When I did finally take the camera out of the box, I was completely intimidated. This was too much camera for me. I was even a little bit angry. This was obviously a camera intended for someone with skill, knowledge, and experience. I didn't have any of those things. I just liked to take pictures. It wasn't enough to justify the expense. If the children hadn't had a hand in picking it out, I might have even insisted it be returned.

They were so excited. I couldn't disappoint them.

Eventually, I got used to the idea. I had always enjoyed taking photos, and the advent of the digital age meant that I could do it without the prohibitive cost of film and developing. The world opened up in that moment.

It was a difficult time. I was running a business, fighting for my children, all the while dealing with an uncooperative and unreliable husband. I felt like I was drowning, fighting for air. I was a rat in a cage, constantly spinning my wheel and not gaining any ground. The continued pressure was beginning to take a toll on me, and I couldn't afford for that to happen. My children needed me to be there for them. They were lost and confused; their father had all but quit on them. They needed to know that there was a steady force in their lives — someone they could count on. That someone was me. I knew I had to take a step back, gain some perspective. I needed to clear my head. At last, an idea began to form.

What if I were to take a day — just one day — and get away from everyone? I didn't have another scheduled visit with the kids for a few days. I could take my journal, my new camera, pack a lunch, and spend the day alone, with no phone. There was a park in the city that I had visited once before. It was there that I learned about the red-winged blackbird. I had never seen one, but the more I thought about it, the more I wanted to see one, maybe even take a picture. I began to formulate a plan.

The next day dawned bright and clear. I had my camera, my journal, and my picnic all set to go. I knew that once I got away from everything, I could listen to my heart instead of the voices coming at me from all sides. It was exactly what I needed. But as I prepared to leave, my husband showed up at the house. He was having one of his less crazy moments and wanted to have a serious discussion. I could feel the panic building in my chest. I was so close! I couldn't do this right now. This was the only window of time available to me. The next few weeks were fully booked. I needed to be alone. In spite of having spent very little time alone in my life, I knew this to the depths of my being.

My husband paused and looked at me.

"Are you okay?"

"It's just… there's a bird. I've got to… I have to go find the bird!" I was weeping and not making any sense, but for some reason, maybe because crazy recognizes crazy, my husband understood.

"Well, go then! But we really need to talk. Call me later."

I got in my car and pulled away. I made it.

I set my blanket under a large, shady elm in the park, opened up my indulgent lunch of smoked salmon, strawberries, and brie, and wrote in my journal for two solid hours. Everything I hadn't been able to say, everything I thought, I felt, I dreamed — all of it came out in the first cathartic purging of my soul. I sat back and breathed deeply. I was starting to feel better. Now, to find that bird.

It wasn't going to be easy. There were birds — a few black-capped chickadees and a white-breasted nuthatch, but no red-winged blackbirds. Truthfully, I didn't know the names of any of them; I just knew they weren't the ones I was looking for. For the next three hours, I walked around the marsh, taking pictures of the wildflowers, the marsh grasses, the ducks on the pond… I couldn't identify any of those either.

It didn't matter. What mattered was I had become so involved in what I was doing that for the first time in months, I wasn't thinking about my problems. I was completely relaxed. Everything had become clear. It was exhilarating.

I had broken the yoke that had me chained to events outside my control. It was a revelation.

The search for the red-winged blackbird didn't end there. It was almost a year before I finally saw one. But the quest became synonymous with finding myself. For the first time in my life, I realized the value of self care and understood that in order for me to be my best, I had to be at my best. I began to spend more time out with my camera. I realized that I enjoyed my own company, in some cases more that the company I'd been keeping. I started to filter those relationships out of my life. I bought guidebooks and started to learn the names of the birds and the flowers. I began to be a person, not just a boss, a wife, or a mother. I had found a way to be whole.

I fought back and my kids were returned to me. The marriage was taped back together, and fell apart a few years later, when I was better equipped to deal with it. Throughout it all, I made time for myself, my camera, and my search for the red-winged blackbird. It seems strange to think that a camera could do all of that for a person, but sometimes in life, you just need to adjust your focus.

I'm still learning.

Honourable Mention — **Nonfiction**

This story embodied the emotional personal journey of a broken woman who finds peace and life meaning from an unexpected (and self-described, undeserved) gift. The author has centred on the main character and draws the reader into her world of despair and pain. As a reader, I wanted her to succeed in all aspects of her story. I found that "In Search of the Red-Winged Blackbird" was a story of self-exploration that did go full circle. A job well done.

— Faye Arcand

THE WELCOMIN'

DAVID A. POULSEN

I suppose I must've been standin' there about an hour and a half when I saw the train sort of lumbering down the track toward us. It was a cold day too, so actually I guess it was the steam I saw first.

January's always the coldest month in southern Saskatchewan, and that particular January, the one that got 1943 off and rolling, was a beaut. Still, I bet half of Swift Current was right there on that platform waitin' for that train to arrive, and me with 'em.

Even the town band was out and all dressed up in their uniforms. They'd already played a couple of tunes, you know, to give the whole thing a little atmosphere, like a celebration. It probably helped to keep 'em from freezin' to death too, in those uniforms. There wasn't a whole lot to 'em. I imagine they mostly got used in the summer for parades and stuff like that.

I mean it was a celebration. What else do you call it when two war heroes are being welcomed home?

I'd had a lot of time to think about the whole thing — I mean wars and heroes and all that — while I'd been standin' there on the platform. I'd thought a lot about how I remembered Ray Harmon and Orrie Franchuk, too, before they left for the war, especially when I saw "Hammer" Hammermeister on the platform.

I couldn't believe it. Hammer Hammermeister in Swift Current to welcome back his two worst enemies.

It was seeing him standin' there shiverin' like the rest of us that really started me thinking, you know, remembering.

I guess when you start remembering stuff about somebody special in your life, you just naturally go back to a time that really stands out. You know, like when you're thinkin' about your dad, you automatically remember the time he brought home a puppy and had it hid in a box so you couldn't see it, and he walks in all casual and says, "Hey, anybody know where I should put this box of books? Oh, guess right here'll be okay," he says, and then he sets the box down and there's a puppy in there, not books at all, and you wanna kiss him but you can't because when you're nine years old there's some things you just can't do.

Well, that's about the way it was for me with Ray Harmon and Orrie Franchuk. The special time I remember about them was just about two years before that day on the train platform. It was the most important hockey game of my life, maybe the most important hockey game in the whole history of Swift Current.

The Beavers were playin' the Elrose Flyers, and as much as it's possible for a seven-year-old kid to hate is how much I hated the Flyers.

You wouldn't have believed that game. I mean you have to realize that the winner would be heading off to Ottawa to play their team for the national championship. All season long the Beavers and the Flyers had been really close. They'd beaten us twice, we beat them once, and we tied 'em once.

And now here it was — the game — and we were losing 2–1 in the third period. We scored our goal while Hammermeister was in the penalty box. He was usually good for two or three penalties and maybe a fight every game.

He had one of their goals as well. I mean, Hammermeister was a great player, there was no denyin' that, but he was so dirty, and on top of that he was from Elrose, so there was no way you could keep from hatin' the guy.

So there we were with seven minutes left in the game and me screamin' my lungs out in the bleachers. My dad who didn't get excited about stuff was sittin' up kind of tall and watchin' everything real close, and even mom had quit talkin' to Iris Oldfield in the row behind us and was actually payin' attention to the game.

And then sure enough, there was Hammer Hammermeister livin' up to his name and practically runnin' one of our guys through the boards. Only the ref caught him, and Hammermeister was gone for another two minutes.

I knew this was it. We had to get one during this penalty or we could forget all about Ottawa. I guess our guys knew it too, because Ray Harmon made a great play to get around one of their defencemen and slid a pass in front to his winger, and just like that it was 2–2.

Boy, did I give it to Hammermeister as he was comin' out of the penalty box, but I doubt if he heard me. The noise in that place was unbelievable.

Then came the most exciting five minutes of my life. With about two minutes to go, Ray Harmon stole the puck from one of their defencemen, faked the goalie right out of his socks, and bingo, it was 3–2 for the Beavers.

But the thing wasn't over, not by a long shot. Now, you wouldn't think a team leading by one goal with less than a minute left in the game would allow the other team a breakaway, would you? Sure enough, though, thirty seconds to go and suddenly, who's got the puck and is headin' in on goal but Hammer Hammermeister. Orrie Franchuk was our goalie and he'd been playin' great all game, and I remember prayin' real quick that he had one more save in him. I remember how I promised God I'd never say "damn" again at least until I was twenty-one if he'd let Orrie make that save. It's funny how your mind works at a time like that.

Anyway, Hammermeister let go a shot, and one thing I'll say about Hammer Hammermeister, he had about the hardest shot I've ever seen. I don't know how Orrie could've seen the shot, maybe he didn't, but somehow he got his glove over there and sure enough, the puck was in that glove. I couldn't believe it, no kidding, I just couldn't. I think it was bedtime that night before my heart sort of got back to beatin' normal.

And now here's Hammer Hammermeister standin' on that platform, waiting for Ray and Orrie to get down off that train. It was funny… I tried to picture Orrie and Ray over there fightin' the Germans; it was a place called Dieppe, somewhere or other in France, and every time I tried to picture a German in my mind he'd look like Hammer Hammermeister.

The train was coming closer. People were starting to kind of push forward, so I did too 'cause I wanted to make real sure I could see those guys. I could see Ray Harmon's mom and dad, smiling away and moving up to the edge of the platform. I have to admit I was gettin' pretty excited myself. Maybe not quite as much as when the Beavers beat the Flyers but almost.

The train finally stopped and the band started playin' like crazy. Only thing is, they played for about ten minutes and nobody got off the train. Nothing happened. Finally the band quit playing and everybody just stood around looking at the train and at each other like they didn't know what they were supposed to do next.

Then just about the time everybody was getting ready to give up and go home, Ray Harmon came into the doorway of the train. Except, it wasn't Ray Harmon, you know what I mean?

The guy that was in the doorway of that train car was leaning on crutches because one of his legs was gone. His right arm was all bandaged up too. I thought that was strange because the battle had been months before, and I figured a person would have healed up in that time.

But the worst part was his face. I mean, I remember seein' that face with the biggest grin on it you ever saw after that goal against Elrose. But as he was coming down off that train, Ray's face didn't look like it had ever grinned, and maybe never would again. I don't know if I'm explaining it exactly right. It was like he was dead, only his body was still alive.

They brought him down off the train and Ray's mom and dad and two guys who looked sort of like doctors led him through the crowd. They came right by me, and I swear Ray Harmon looked right at me but he never said anything or even let on that he knew me or anything. I figured at the time maybe he hadn't seen me after all.

It was awful quiet just then. The band guys were standin' there holding their instruments and tryin' to keep warm and nobody seemed to feel much like celebratin' anymore.

Then another doctor-lookin' guy was standing in the doorway of the train and he was holding onto Orrie Franchuk. Orrie had this big bandage across his eyes and I heard a couple of women say, "Oh my God," and one guy behind me said, "Why didn't they let us know us it was like this?"

Of course it was later that we found out the truth about Dieppe. It was a lot different from what we'd been reading and hearing from all those war correspondents.

Orrie and Ray were with the South Saskatchewan Regiment that attacked a place called Pourville. We learned that Orrie only made it about fifty yards up the beach and behind a sea wall. Then he got pinned down by machine gun fire for about four hours. Never moved. Never fired a shot. He lost his eyes when he finally made a dash back to the water and a bullet ricocheted off the landing-boat thing he was trying to get into and hit him.

Ray Harmon was quite a ways from Orrie, and he got past the beach and up to this bridge. A lot of guys never made it across that bridge, and Ray Harmon was one of the ones who didn't. He'd laid there holding onto his leg trying to keep it from falling off for about two hours before the medics were able to get to him.

Seein' those guys like that, I don't know, it sort of got to me.

But you know the strangest thing about that day at the train station? After they led Orrie through the crowd, I turned around and Hammer Hammermeister was standin' there cryin'. I don't mean a little tear in the corner of his eye; the man was practically bawlin'. I mean, I was too, but you expect that from a little kid. But Hammer Hammermeister with tears streamin' down his face?

They never had any more welcomin's for war heroes after that. Maybe that was just as well. It didn't turn out to be much of a celebration anyway.

ME AND THE **PIGEON** IN **TUSCANY**

WENDY WESEEN

Here in a small café
I talk to a pigeon
picking its way
across the back of a red chair
Pretend he is my lost husband
"Aren't you sorry you're not here?

"You could have had egg salad sandwiches.
This wine is so sweet. It tastes like a flower.
You should have seen the nifty tool at the market
The one that does ten things
even bought it
You would have loved the graffiti on the canal wall
fishermen in moored boats
cleaning their decks
shucking their shells.
You could have reached for my hand.
Found me."

SECOND-PLACE WINNER — **POETRY**

This poem is a homily on the transference of grief to metaphors of hope, as the writer, who is on a journey of recovery, transposes past to present. We are familiar with birds as symbols of the spirit, the however-many grams of soul that leave the body in death or the heart in the loss of a relationship. In a simple moment, in a café, the writer is assured by the presence of a bird she can talk to that the conversation continues beyond the boundaries of loss. Venturing beyond, the narrator returns us to home, where the heart is.

— Linda Rogers

Li'l **Old**

Debbie Pakka

"Old Lady..."

No... I think I'll call you "Li'l Old." That'll be my name for you, 'cause first off, I don't know your real name. And second thing... when I noticed you... small and frail... I knew you were the perfect target... "So little... so old..."

So I'm gonna name you after that first impression.

Well, Li'l Old... there's no going back now.

It's a strange thing to me, that I wanna give you some kind of a name. I can't make sense of it. I only know that ever since our brief encounter a few days ago, I can't seem to shake you off. You're always in my head now, constantly feeding this relentless loop inside my subconscious. Somehow, you've set up residence in my tortured mind — and I say the word "tortured" 'cause that's what it is. Tortured and angry.

They say I've always been a big boy for my age, but at sixteen, I now stand six feet five inches tall. I tower above the rest, especially you, Li'l Old. But you know this 'cause you've met me once before.

My stocky build and muscular frame intimidate the world around me, and the tattoos on my neck and arms are ugly and menacing. Menacing like me.

My old man tells me everyday I'm a screw-up, but I figure I can't be all that dense, 'cause I can tell you exactly what goes on inside every disapproving, inflated head that darts by me. You see, to them, Li'l Old, I'm nothing but dog mess that's been smeared across the sidewalk, to be sidestepped around; given a wide berth; while faces try and fail to hide their looks of contempt and disgust. Oh, there's fear in their eyes too, but I know what they're thinking. Dirtbag! Oxygen thief!

I can feel it, way down… deep inside.

And I try, Li'l Old, not to give a damn. Trying only gets you so far though…

You can't possibly know this, but I've been watchin' you for days now. I've made a mental note of your comings and goings, and what I'm about to do is making me nervous. Roller coaster, gut-gripping nervous. The act of it, so foreign to me that it's clouding and confusing my brain. Not that I have much of a brain to confuse.

You see, Li'l Old, if I did have one — a brain, that is — I certainly wouldn't know it, let alone believe it. The old man stole that idea from me a long time ago by worming his way into my skull… and when someone hijacks the very essence of your being… well, you kinda become what you're told, right?

So, who am I then?

I'm Danny Dumpster, the dummy son of a mean, bitter fool; a fool with a temper so hot, he's always wild and crazy, like a rabid raccoon caught in a live trap. I mean it when I say it, that when he leaves this poor excuse of an existence he's called life, it won't matter to me… not one bit. And just for the record, Li'l Old, I think I might be turning into my old man… or maybe into something worse…

It's interesting to me that you aren't aware of my presence, but then again, I've always been careful to keep to the shadows. My hands are idle except for the occasional clenching, while yours, Li'l Old, move with a flurry, your gardening gloves tattered and worn in contrast to your new yellow-brimmed hat. When I notice you slowly rise up from the rose garden to stroll over to the lilac bush in your yard, I awaken with a sense of urgency. I watch as you bend the purple-flowered cluster close to your chin and breathe in its sweet scent. You are distracted and my mind commands me to move swiftly now. "Just do it!" it says, but the glare of daylight exposes my weakness. I am too afraid! I lose the nerve but not the will.

I will come tonight instead, while you sleep, covered in your blankets; me covered in a blanket of darkness…

As I wait for nightfall, it gives me plenty of time to think back to the day I first saw you. I remember carefully making my way to the front of the bus where you were sitting, my eyes never leaving the purse at your side. I watched and calculated your every move, like a cougar stalking its prey. I needed a victim… a victim just like you, Li'l Old. I needed to steal your money, but even more, I needed to rob you of your joy; the joy I was convinced everyone else in the world was feeling that day… but me.

I needed you to feel my anguish… I wanted someone… anyone… to know my pain…

It's midnight now, Li'l Old, and I'm three blocks from your house. I don't feel as jumpy inside as I thought I would, and I kinda feel all right, like I'm about to get some form of release. I wasn't always this way. I'm not what I seem… I'm not!

Then who am I really?

I'm Danny, the trembling five-year-old, weeping in his bed, crying desperately, night after night, for a wayward mother who left and never returned. I'm Danny, the seven-year-old with the stinging, red-rimmed eyes, stubbornly holding back tears and anger as school bullies taunt with the cruelest of nicknames, "Danny Dumpster!" The very nickname hatched by a father who claimed, to anyone who would listen, that the kid he was forced to call son should've been "thrown in the trash the day he was born…"

I'm Danny, whose dark and hardened eyes are a contradiction to the anguished look of terror that used to belong to the nine-year-old boy with the racing heart, hiding beneath the bed and pleading for mercy from the one who should have been his mentor and rock… his guiding hand. I'm Danny, lost and damaged. And yet when I look in the mirror now, I see a tiny crumb, just a hint of worth in my reflection. And it's all 'cause of you, Li'l Old.

It's still so clear, so vivid… the rush of adrenaline, my sinister reach from behind to knock the handbag from your shoulder, the failed attempt, the beautiful sweetness in your eyes as you turned on your heels to face me, and the unbelievable, unthinkable moment… when you asked for my help. What made you do it?

I remember standing there in stunned silence as you passed me your purse along with the small bag of groceries you had been carrying. When you turned your back to me, to work the hinge on your gate, I couldn't believe my luck! I felt the dire, pressing sensation to run, to break away, take advantage of a stupid, crazy old lady. But my legs disobeyed and kept me anchored to the sidewalk. I was spellbound, rooted to the spot while holding on to the very thing I had wanted to take, but now, could not.

I remember the image of you, Li'l Old, the face of the gentle grandmother I often conjured up in my boyhood dreams, and as much as I wanted to flee, to bolt, I was unable to escape; graced by the searing, innocent trust in your eyes.

It felt like an eternity before you returned to retrieve the items in my hands and to thank me for the favor. It was then, for a split second, that all the world stood still…

I can still feel the breeze in my hair and the smell of the lilac bush in your yard as I sensed something strange and foreign rise up in my nature, something noble and pure that I'd never felt before. The funny thing is, Li'l Old, I can still feel it, even now… I can!

So tonight I come, in the dark, 'cause the truth of the matter is that even with all the sway and swagger, I'm not brave, not brave at all. And what I really wanna tell you, the stuff I keep inside, well that's gotta wait for another day.

So, I'll just leave this note on your doorstep, with a single rose from your garden to say thank you, Li'l Old… for trustin' and believin' in me when no one else in the world would, and for giving me somethin' I never knew existed… till now. Somethin' I think I'll call… "Hope."

First Place — **Fiction**

I was knocked out with this work. The author took on a couple of difficult challenges — choosing to write in the present tense and in the first person while addressing a second person throughout, and was able to pull off both with great success. The well-crafted story with its thoroughly believable narrating character and relentless building of dread in its tone sets up readers perfectly, and the twist at the end was beautifully handled. As a writer of crime fiction, I'm always delighted when the author is able to put one over on me, and I definitely did not see that end coming. Well done.

— David A. Poulsen

Deep Throat

Linda Rogers

We did it when we were kids. "Is your refrigerator running?" "Yes," came the trembling affirmative. "Well, go catch it then." And then the killer, the one that gave my grandmother, married to an Athole of that ilk, my Scottish grandfather, Athole Black of the Black Rod, her first mild stroke. "Is your asshole black?"

We were hilarious, made ourselves wet ourselves when telephones were toys, long before I borrowed a cell and called my now-dead friend across the dinner table and asked him to pass the salt on a borrowed cell phone.

That friend has gone to the land of longest distance and I wonder if he took his phone with him, and if he did, does it work? Does he call his wife for phone sex? Does he dial up the artist list on his Rolodex and arrange house concerts for the big concert hall in the sky? I should look into that now that there are more rock stars in heaven than there are on Earth.

It would be nice to hitch a ride on a Virgin flight to Mars, where the craters make natural amphitheatres and there might be natural congress between the living and the dead. Imagine, one more go around with the Beatles, with Jimi Hendrix, or a Nirvana reunion? The list is endless. That is a cliché for good reason, like all clichés, and what is more clichéd than old rockers, even the ones that die young?

If my social information is correct and our neighbour Lewis is "Lewis" as the result of an accident rather than a bad fairy kiss at birth, he almost went there. Rumour has it he was a chef at the Empress Hotel, on his way to chess grand master, authorship of Beatles songs, and a fourth job as the Great One's enforcer before his alleged head injury. Everything now is BHI and AHI, just like Jesus, he has his acronyms, only AHI is no joke. It has him confined to the special needs residence across the street and tethered to memories that wander between forgotten and made up, all of them kind.

The only part that is not made up into parables is the one about chess, and this Lewis can prove with newspaper clippings. Once a week he takes the bus downtown and beats the ass off every other player at the Kiwanis Lodge. The *Times-Colonist*, locally known as the *Tums-Colonic*, printed pictures of Lewis with lots of game timers and multiple players, all of them wearing dazed expressions of vicarious brilliance, blessed in the blood of an accident victim.

Our neighbour Lewis has many awesome talents. In addition to the spatial and logistic skills necessary for board combat, he is able to navigate the five-mile radius around his care home with a limp and a cane, price check at least half a dozen grocery stores, and be home in time for his daily Lewis report before lunch is served at 11:30 on the dot, today burritos and tater tots. The Lewis report, his own commodities index, compares strawberries in and out of season, winter pansies, and twelve-packs of Coca-Cola. He has a limited repertoire, but within it, he is fastidious.

Lewis brings drawings for the children to colour, but he will not be hugged by anyone, child or otherwise. Hugging always gets the same response, a sort of shrink tremor, arms glued to his sides, making himself if not invisible, then at least thin enough to vanish between cracks in the sidewalk. Lewis enjoys transubstantiation, his elusive genius. Could be someone almost squeezed him to death, but he'll never tell.

We have speculated about the hugging, the savant information gathering and disseminating, the chess, divine intelligence, but none of it adds up because we're missing key pieces. And we don't ask him because of the don't-ask/don't-tell policy and the rules across the street, which are pretty much the same as the rules at William Head prison, where we pay Sunday visits to inmates. Never ask how they got there.

Here are some other possibilities: While dreaming, Lewis walked in front of a bus, while protecting the Great One, or Lewis was bully-barrelled into the boards head first, or while scoring lyrics for John Lennon in the woods at a top-ranking golf course, Lewis was struck by lightning or a random bogie, or Lewis slipped on a banana peel in the Empress Hotel kitchen. Sometimes I wonder if he was ever really there.

Lewis had one vice, which he quit cold turkey after I bullied the city into building a smoking garden at the home. There is a no-smoking rule in the home and outside within a perimeter that reaches to the sidewalk, leaving not one square inch for the inmates to loiter and puff. I am against smoking, allergic actually to cigarette smoke, which is filthier than even than the average physician's necktie, but for compassionate reasons, some rules need to be tossed.

All the guys across the street puffed like steam engines. Puffing and sucking was comfort and sport. I swear they competed to complete as many fag ends as they could find in ashtrays and gutters and sometimes — Oh happy day! — real boxes of real cigarettes.

The Lewis Report was as regular as rain in this cloud-infested city of turbulent weather. Nothing interfered with Lewis's lifetime commitment to competitive pricing. Nothing except smoking. Funny he never quoted cigarette prices. I know for a fact they are cheaper on the res, which charges no taxes, but that is a story for another day, one possibly beyond Lewis's five-mile repertoire.

And by now you have noticed I switched to past tense. Smoke and mirrors.

The problem was, the boys were forced to sit on the curb to do their rituals, rolling and smoking, legs hanging out on the street, live bait for charging minivans and motorcycles.

"You are begging for amputees!" I shrieked at the home, and just as fast as we picked up lawn chairs at yard sales and thrift shops and placed them on the boulevard, staff removed them. There had to be a way, I told Lewis in our many late-night phone calls, he, I imagine, hiding with his phone under his institutional sheets and me awakened by nightmares of neighbourhood dogs delivering special-needs feet to our front porch.

You may also have noticed that I am a we. Married. Attached to the old ball and chain. Sort of. Our minds wander, but our bodies spoon with predictable regularity.

Recently, he found some old negatives and, using his not-yet-dormant science skills, was able to reverse them using a cardboard construction, reflected light, and his phone. Don't ask. That comes up a lot, doesn't it? When he spread the prints across our kitchen table, adjacent to a particularly fine bowl of mushroom risotto, I choked on fifty-year-old photos of his first wife rendered from negative to positive — in short, a babe.

When Lewis first appeared at our door to ask for bottles, then began to phone several times daily, but always in daytime, I started calling him "The Boyfriend" just to see if that registered on the green scale. It didn't. My husband, with whom I share everything from geriatric intimacy to chocolates (we bite them in half), is supremely confident that he has control of both my conscious and subconscious minds. I know he will read this because he reads my email every morning and evening, and I'm sure his fingers wander over to the word app. Why wouldn't they? He tells me I have a fascinating mind every time I ask him if he still thinks I am gorgeous, like the ripe taleggio cheese I adore.

Old people become habitual. Across the street is our regular television. We sit on the front porch and watch. Sometimes we have beer and peanuts. Really. There is constant drama in the garden, regular attendance by cops and ambulances, and then the beautiful mad girl who takes fifty steps north then forty south where she stands still as the cheese in the middle, as if posing for some cosmic photo shoot. Here I am. Come and get me. I am crazy beautiful, queen of the random universe.

I am not by and large a manipulative person, but I am curious and I never change the channel. When it serves my purpose, I do due diligence. I pay attention. I make cookies and pies. And, naturally, I am pals with the gardener, who told me in a confiding moment over a clump of rescue dandelions (he agrees with me that dandelions are bee food and need to be protected no matter the status quo in our middle-class neighbourhood, rife with rowers and dog walkers who "own" the surrounding park) that the home actually has no jurisdiction over the boulevard, the sidewalk, and a three-foot band of disputed territory.

"Busted." I am not the sister and daughter etcetera of ruthless criminal lawyers for nothing. I have their skills, only instead of defending the greedy and guilty, my clientele is language challenged. Lewis has speech deficits, but I spoke up for the smokers, harassing City Hall and the Health Authority, and voila! One fine day, the cement mixer came and laid down a smokers' patio, right in line with the one-yard allowance, the sidewalk, and the boulevard.

"I had to quit," he whispered on the phone one night. "No more smokes. Nurse Chin Hairs took them."

Fine. I did it for him, but not just for him. The residents were once a pack of happy smokers, but Lewis disappeared, giving them a berth as wide as the road to smoker's hell. He vanished for a month and, when he came back like the cat in the song, repaired and depuffed, disinhaled, I never once saw him sit with the boys and girls who also quit cold rooster and now sit in the circle of garden chairs and pebbled concrete they call prayer group.

Had Lewis seen a proverbial ghost and taken a break while they made up their own minds? Just like the chess games, "the visit" as it came to be known, his clandestine disappearance was the deep state equivalent to our deep throat conversations at night, most of them unintelligible, Lewis mumbling and me yelling at him to speak up.

"Where did you go?" I asked. "Did you all actually quit smoking?"

"Strawberries $2.95 a box, primroses 99 cents," he whispered *sotto voce*, and maybe in denial or sheer stupidity (my ex called me thick as cardboard when I left) I never suspected he had given up his walks and, using the light from his phone, was lying in the dark, reading to me from a flyer or maybe holy scripture.

Lewis was, to all intents and purposes, living like a monk: no walkabouts, no Mexican strawberries, no fags. *But he never told me why or how.*

His visits stopped, but not the phone calls. I stopped calling him my boyfriend and my husband suggested, "The Patient." Hadn't he been patient after all, standing on our front porch in the middle of the night with handfuls of flowers he'd picked in random gardens, the sometimes-cold tater tots wrapped in grocery flyers from feasts across the street, or printed drawings of Easter bunnies and Valentine hearts to colour with crayons? So what was different now?

I began diagramming, first the missing brain parts, then a heart, a lung, whatever. Never mind, Lewis was erasing himself, just like the Cheshire Cat, who disappeared, all but his smile. Only with Lewis, it was his voice, once a mumble jumble of stuttered consonants and now just lonely vowels, sound of the wind blowing through the trees that separate the special needs house from ours.

"Luhluhluh, maybe 'Love, love, love.' "

Now Lewis, smoke free, incandescent, knew the value of everything, and possibly the price of nothing. Isn't that enlightenment?

I went across the street to check on him, but the bitch of a nurse, Ms. Chin Hairs, filling the door with her malign aura only told me, "He's sleeping."

Of course he was napping. He'd been up all night, sending Lewis code to the universe.

Slowly, Lewis's vowels slipped into darkness. The calls had been coming in the middle of the night 3 a.m., four a.m. My husband, who actually hears the high-pitched rings in his sleep, took the phone off the hook, but the messages stacked up.

"Who is it?" I asked when he checked the phone in the morning

"I don't know, it's all zeros."

"Could it be Lewis?"

"Not his number. More likely a call company in India."

"Can you stop them?"

They stopped themselves, and one afternoon, masses of beautiful white-with-blush Princess Diana roses appeared like a drift of snow on our welcome mat. No delivery man. No knock at the door, no note.

I know their provenance, just a long distance call away. We've watched the documentaries. In countries where there isn't enough water for thirsty populations, no toilets and no washing of clothes, flowers packed in cocaine are grown for the very rich and flown around the world. They are very expensive. Our roses were perky and happy, on a contact high. No wonder they looked so fresh. I admit this is what I was thinking when I unwrapped them.

"Did somebody die?" my husband asked.

"You'd think so," I answered, "but who?"

"Maybe they came from God." My husband is an atheist, but he does talk to someone when he meditates.

I put the long-stemmed blooms in water, filling several large vases. We had roses in every room: the living room, our bedroom, the kitchen, even the bathroom.

There was only one call after that. That evening. Not late, but almost.

"Kisses zero, hugs zero, the circle of love," clear as a bell. Lewis spoke very carefully, like a tennis linesman during a tense match, and then he hung up.

I ran across the street in my nightie, barefoot in the rain: no coat, no shoes.

"I need to see Lewis," I said, firmly, to Chin Hairs, that nurse, when she came to the door, smelling of cigarettes.

"Lewis is gone."

"Where?"

"Gone, the funeral was today. It was private," she said, lifting her weight on her toes, making her big shadow bigger.

"But he called me just now," I protested.

"No, he didn't." I'd never liked her. She was the one we called the enforcer, who made sure the patients sat on the curb to smoke because rules were rules, who opposed the prayer-for-merly-smoking garden with regulations.

"I actually hate you, and, for the record, Lewis does too," I said.

"Did," she said. "Lewis did hate me. That's why I'm here. I am not his mother. Was not," she corrected herself.

"So you sent the flowers to the wrong address."

"Only the bill. He ordered the roses, and, of course, he had no money."

Weeks have passed since that nasty interaction. It is true, Lewis is gone, and we never did get the bill for the roses he sent. Of course we didn't.

Did I mention they called me "The Witch" at school because I foreshadowed like crazy? All my stories came true.

Need I tell you that, on the shortest night in the year, winter solstice, Nurse Chin Hairs sat down on the icy curb and nodded off with one of Lewis's confiscated cigarettes hanging from her lips? It was reported in the newspaper, but I had already felt the shiver, heard the screech of tires at midnight and witnessed frozen blood, the colour of the blossoms on our red chestnut tree, on porch TV the next morning. She wouldn't have dared to sit in the smoking garden after opposing it so vigorously. Bad karma.

Lewis is gone, but the taste of strawberries past lingers in our kisses, and his incoherent prayers whisper in the branches of our red chestnut tree.

"He knew the value of everything." We say our prayers before falling asleep, the pronoun he in for "Him," inviting him into our dreams, his arms full of X's and O's. "Now it is our turn."

MRS. M. COX'S **MEAT ROLL**

NANCY DAVIES

Mari talks in her sleep. I discovered this when we shared a room on a two-week bus tour of Britain. We set out from a budget hotel in Earl's Court, lumbering in a diesel fog up to the Lake District, through Scotland, down to Penzance, into the New Forest and, finally, Wales. Mari was tiny, with a pronounced widow's hump. When you walked behind her it looked like she had no head. She was eighty-nine. She was my aunt.

We had a cream tea in Bath and passed a Land Rover with a royal crest on a country road near Balmoral. "That was Prince Philip," said our guide who was the spitting image of Steve Martin, and everyone *Oooed*. We saw gardens, castles, country houses, Stonehenge. "We've seen plenty of ruins," said Peter, one of two hearty, thirtyish Australian brothers who had inexplicably chosen a tour full of old people to see Britain. "And some of them are on this bus!" Luckily Mari was hard of hearing.

She wanted to see "the old country" one last time.

I knew little of her private life. She had few friends. Mari's parents left Wales in the early 1920s for a new life on the Alberta prairie, where they raised their two children — Mari and her older brother David, my father. Mari's mother cooked from the *Blue Ribbon Cookbook*, found in every prairie kitchen and usually annotated with recipes from the local women's church group. Mari would laugh, recalling the nearly inedible meals: thin soups, cracker gruel, plain milk toast. We laughed too about my mother's terrible cooking — prepared using her mother's copy of the same cookbook. At the age of nine, I stuck a handwritten recipe for popcorn snowballs in amongst the tips for "restoring tainted game" and overcoming its wild flavor.

I knew Mari dreamed of distant places, of French food, of living in Paris. Instead she led a quiet, solitary life, working as a clerk for the provincial government out of high school until her retirement, and living with her widowed father until he died when she was nearing fifty. French food was never more than a quiche at White Spot.

It was clear the trip was too much for her, daily packing and unpacking, struggling with unfamiliar showers. I could hear her frustration through the bathroom door, but she refused any help. She wanted to maintain her independence and I understood. But I worried that the trip disappointed her. I wanted it to be memorable. I didn't know how to make it better, and she remained quiet. I began starting the shower for her in the mornings, for which I believe she was wordlessly grateful.

We kept the same bus seats for the duration of the trip. The man in front of me had a full head of white hair and a profile much like my father's. I would study the back of his head and think, *Help me, dad. I don't know what I'm doing.*

Mari spent most of the time on the bus asleep, nodding and snoring through the green sheep-dotted downs, past lochs, through foggy heathered hills, big cities and market towns. For her, the draw of the trip was a two-hour stop in the Welsh town of Builth Wells, where for generations her family had kept a shop. When we arrived there I woke her and we walked to find it. Now a Spar — the equivalent of a 7-Eleven — the inside was clinical, white with accents of green, lit by fluorescent lights. "My aunt's family used to have a store here," I said to the disinterested young woman behind the counter. Between us in a glass case, a wheel of withered hot dogs circled slowly under a heat lamp. I looked at Mari. She looked away. Later in our hotel room she asked if there had been sheep on the hills. I said there had. "I wonder how I missed them," she said.

Not long after we returned home, Mari became ill. I was spending nights in Victoria at her condo, sleeping in her spare room on a hide-a-bed no one but me had ever slept on. I would often wake to Mari in full voice. "Whaaaaaat?" she would shout. "No! I don't want to go to the pool hall with you! Why don't you ever take me someplace nice, like the movies? And you're married!" One night there were softer sounds, like mewing. I went into her room, said, "Mari?" "Oh," she said, with frightened eyes. "Oh!" I called 911.

Her heart was bad and she'd contracted C. difficile, which had weakened her further. "Let her go," said the harried hospital doctor. "What kind of life will she have? She'll end up in bed in an institution. She needs a feeding tube, and a needle into her heart. She's ninety. It's too much for her."

"What should I do?" Mari asked me simply. "Should I just go?"

Help me, dad. I don't know what I'm doing.

I remembered the doctor said he'd given her a stronger antibiotic to fight the infection. "Why not take the weekend to see if it works?" I said. She thought a moment and said, "Yes. Yes, I can do that."

Next day, she was hooked up to half a dozen bleeping, blinking, buzzing machines. She had a feeding tube and a needle into her heart. She had made her decision. When I visited her in the weeks that she was in hospital, the first thing she'd say was always, "And how are you?"

"I'm all right, but how are *you*," I'd ask, and she was fine. Always fine.

A few weeks later, she was home. I found home care during the day and resumed nights on the lumpy hide-a-bed.

I'd been volunteering at St. Vincent de Paul in Sooke a few days a week, sorting book donations — endless John Grisham and James Patterson, Janet Evanovich and Patricia Cornwell, near-pristine boxed sets of *Twilight* and *Fifty Shades of Grey*. The staff were fun and supportive. "How's your aunt?" Carey would ask. "She's okay, but I don't know what the hell I'm doing!" I'd say, and we'd laugh. Then I'd drive to Victoria for night duty to be woken regularly at 3 a.m. by Mari in full voice. "No! I won't go to the beer parlour with you! Whaaaat? Say that to your wife!"

"Look at this old cookbook," Carey said, holding out a tattered, yellowed thing with a faded blue ribbon on its dirty cover. She said she'd felt the need to keep it aside for me but didn't know why.

Was it possible? "There might be a recipe for popcorn snowballs in there," I said, and opening it, there it was. And in my grandmother's handwriting in pencil on the inside cover, another wonderfully terrible recipe.

Mrs. M. Cox's Meat Roll
Grind 8 lbs beef and about 1 1/2 lbs of bacon.
Add salt and pepper and mix well.
Pack into baking powder tins and boil for 3 hrs.
Pour off liquid and cover well with fat.

My parents had been dead for sixteen years. Where had this book been, and how did it come to me now?

Then it was time for Mari to go into a home. We spent hours a day at her condo, sorting and deciding what to keep.

In her large bedroom bureau were gloves, letters, birthday cards, wedding announcements, every pair of glasses she'd ever owned, the bottom two inches from every pair of pants she'd shortened (a whole drawer of these), decades worth of scarves and necklaces I'd bought her for Christmas. All carefully examined and in the end, she decided, thrown out. Except for one scarf I gave her when I was a teenager. A silk print with a bronze, blue, and pink paisley. When I bought it I thought it was the most beautiful scarf I'd ever seen, and I still do.

A few days after Mari had moved into her new place, a care worker with an engraved brass name tag that read *Linda* said, "Your aunt is lovely, isn't she?" and I said, "Yes she is," because she is, and because I imagined she would be the perfect resident — quiet, uncomplaining, compliant. But Linda continued, "Did you know, um, that your aunt talks in her sleep?" We both failed at keeping straight faces. "I sure do," I said, and we laughed.

Mari of quiet waters. Mari of raging rivers.

SECOND-PLACE WINNER — **NONFICTION**

This touching story takes us on a journey to learn both the visible story along with the secrets of an elderly woman. The author writes: "Mari was tiny, with a pronounced widow's hump. When you walked behind her it looked like she had no head." Excellent description and introduction, as it not only paints a picture but also allows the reader to draw implied conclusions regarding the life of the woman.

One of the major things in the story used for grounding the story is The Blue Ribbon Cookbook. *This reference again brought the reader right into the farm kitchen and the lives of those there. It brings the story home to the place of recipes and predictability only to allude to the fact that Mari had secrets — as does the cookbook. Well done.*

— Faye Arcand

Dust

Pamela Medland

You are everywhere in our house,
sifted into drawers that stay closed for years,
settled on the tops of books
whose pages I will never open.

Our resident spider remembers you,
or its web does,
the tremor of your step…

In the fall, brown house moths
wrap themselves in another kind of memory,
a white cloud of forgetting
that sleeps through the silence
of winter, awakens in the spring
to the sound of echoes.

First-Place Winner — **Poetry**

"Dust" reverberates in the time of pandemic as we rely on the shared memory of generations to revive the natural world, spiders to weave, every species to lay its eggs in the recesses of our collec-

tive intelligence. The poem is a simple but profound reminder of connections — not just generation to generation, but the phenomenal to the cosmic world we inhabit, as "we sleep through the silence of winter," and awaken to the greater responsibility of corvid spring. Nature reminds us. This poem reminds us in a simple postscriptural way of our intimate and social responsibilities.

— Linda Rogers

The **Dinner**

Océane Picard

Today was the day. Jean pressed her palms on her lap to try and stop the shaking. She had already chewed her fingernails down to the skin. She looked around the table, analyzing every guest and their most likely reaction. Mom would gasp and clasp her hand to her mouth. Dad would look down and shake his head disapprovingly. Probably rub the bridge of his nose. He did that when he was losing patience. Aunt Mary would have the most dramatic reaction. Jean could already hear the sermon she would give: how people like her end up in hell, only redemption could save her. Uncle Jack would remain quiet as usual, and Grandpa would grunt something vaguely offensive and focus back on his food.

Jean exhaled loudly. One of the perks of being sixteen was you could sigh as loud and often as you wanted, and nobody would notice. If they did, they would blame it on the well-known moodiness of teenagers.

"So sweety, tell us about school! Are you keeping good grades?" Aunt Mary asked, snapping Jean back into reality.

"I have something to tell you guys," she began, her voice quiet and unsure.

Aunt Mary turned her attention back to Jean's mother, talking about how great her friend's daughter was doing in some private Christian school. Jean's heart was beating so hard, it seemed impossible nobody heard it. It was time. Waiting would not make it any easier; the sooner it was out, the sooner she could start breathing again. She put her palms on the table and gathered up her strongest voice

"Mom…" she began again. No reaction.

Somehow the conversation had drifted from private schools to the group of refugees moving into town, and everybody seemed to have a heated opinion on the subject.

"Mom, Dad." She said it louder, almost shouting. She had their attention now, too late to back out.

"Mom, Dad, I need to tell you something. I think…" She stopped to take a deep breath. Everybody was staring at her. Just a few more words and she would be done, everything would be out in the open.

"I am bisexual."

The chain of reaction started almost exactly the way she had pictured it. Mom gasped with her eyes wide, Dad looked surprised and somewhat hurt, shaking his head in disbelief. No nose rub yet, which was a good sign. And as expected, dear Auntie started her sermon, infused with a mix of fear and disgust.

"No you are not, Jean! It is the devil talking through your mouth, trying to stir you away from our lord. You need to find Jesus, Jean! I won't let you live a life of sins, of Sodom and Gomorrah! Not in this family! Oh, sweet Jesus, please forgive her, help her find your light." She had closed her eyes, joining her hands in prayer. Her trance-like state was mesmerizing.

"I don't think you are, honey," Jean's Mom said with a soft, worried voice. "I think you are confused. You know… with the media talking about it all the time, it's like a trendy thing to do, but baby..." She grabbed Jean's hand. "It's not real."

These words left a burn on Jean's skin. She had expected her Mom to disagree, to be mad even, but to think she was just following a trend? It was infuriating.

Her dad put his hand on her mother's shoulder.

"Don't worry, Susan. You know it's probably just a phase. Bisexuals are just undecided people, it's not real." He was smiling now. Jean's stomach churned, her heart in her throat.

Aunt Mary jumped at the occasion.

"Real or not, it is still a grave sin! This little phase of yours will send you straight to hell, to burn for eternity! It is not something to take lightly!" Her face was getting red, her voice reaching abnormal heights. "You need to come to mass tomorrow and confess. Father Donovan will be able to help you find the light."

Jean had resolved to remain quiet. Auntie, the saviour of lost souls, would eventually need to catch her breath, and it would be her chance to say something.

"Jesus Christ, Mary, will you cut this crap!"

The loud voice startled everybody. Grandpa had been so quiet, Jean had almost forgotten he was there.

"And you, Susie! Seriously? Your daughter's feelings are not a pair of goddamn bell-bottom pants!"

"Dad!" Mary shrieked at the blasphemy. Susan shot a confused look at her father.

"Dad, are you really going to tell me you're okay with this? Do you believe her?"

The old man closed his eyes and shook his head. Despite being eighty-five, with wispy white hair and a denture, he was a man that still imposed respect. He opened his eyes and smiled.

“Actually Susie, yes. I do believe the kid.” He winked at Jean, who managed a smile despite her surprise.

“And let me tell you something. I’m bisexual too.”

The whole room froze. Jean’s mother spoke first.

“Dad… no…what are you talking about? Mom…”

“I didn’t forget your Mom. How could I? She was the love of my life.”

“Dad, if you’re saying these things just to contradict us, you better stop! It’s not funny!” Aunt Mary hissed.

“I am not,” he simply stated, “There’s plenty you still don’t know about your father.”

“But, Mom…” Jean’s mother repeated. Grandpa raised his hand to stop her.

“Your Mom was my angel, and I loved her. But she wasn’t my first love. I thought I would take these things to the grave, but today seems like a great time to share. Open your stubborn minds,” he said, glancing at both of his daughters with a frown. Jean couldn’t take her eyes away from him. Out of all the ways tonight could have gone, this was definitely the most unexpected. Grandpa cleared his throat.

“I know I’ve already told you about my time in the Vietnam War. How I enlisted when I was twenty because I wanted some adventure, and I thought I could bring pride to my family and my country. Thought I could be a hero.” He paused, the shadows of the past clouding his eyes.

“I enlisted in 1955 and got shipped right away with an American battalion. We were all young, excited, and hopeful. We had no idea what war was. Everything we saw… what we did… it changed us. Our unit consisted of eight soldiers, and I was the only Canadian. We ate, slept, and fought together. James was part of my unit, he was a nineteen-year-old kid from Nebraska. Like me, he wanted to prove he was a man and come home a hero. We got along right away. We understood each other. He was the only thing that kept me going; surviving day after day. He was…" Grandpa stopped and closed his eyes, reliving the painful memories he had buried years ago.

"He was a light in that nightmare of a jungle. We fell in love in the mud between bullets, bugs, and diseases. But at that time, people didn't understand differences in others. You could be shot if they found out you were gay." He shook his head. "The good old days everybody misses so much, huh?" he said with a sarcastic sigh.

"Grandpa, what happened after that?" Jean asked.

"We stayed together for three months. We had planned on running away together, the two of us against the world. A shared dream to help us survive another day. But then…" His voice faltered. "James caught malaria and was sent home. He wrote me letters. Returning home had been awful for him. It wasn't like when we were kids and watched the soldiers come home from France as heroes. People were angry at us. They despised the war." He paused again.

"I got shot two months after James left. I came home and spent a lot of time at the hospital. I was lucky enough, soldiers didn't have the same bad rep in Canada. When I got out, I tried to find him but… the pressure had been too much. A few months after being home, he gave up on life and jumped on the train tracks. I was heartbroken. If I had left the hospital earlier… if I had found him before he…" Grandpa wiped his eyes. "A year later, I started work at the mill and met your mother. She is the only one who knew."

The kitchen clock ticked, the only thing not rendered speechless.

"Dad, I'm so sorry… I didn't know," Jean's mom stammered.

"It's all right, Suze… it's in the past now. But honey. You are lucky enough to have a daughter who is attracted to souls instead of bodies. Don't take that away from her, okay?"
He looked at Jean with a warm, soft smile, and suddenly, she wasn't alone anymore.

Honourable Mention — **Fiction**

I love that in this piece all of the characters behave exactly as one expects — except one. And it's that surprising shift in the reader's expectations that gives this story its power. Strong, believable dialogue gives us strong portrayals of the thoroughly predictable Mom, Dad, and narrow-minded Aunt and the surprisingly unpredictable Grandpa.

— David A. Poulsen

Everyday, Ordinary, Just-After-Work **Sonnet**

Sarah de Leeuw

When you're thinking twice about asking her to dance,
right 'round the living room and through the double-
glass doors, past that now not-so-new granite-topped
kitchen counter you both joked about making love
on, at least once, before dinner, then think again, think
again about your neighbour who hoped he'd heard
ornithology and thought about a rockery of herons
in cottonwood trees when instead the doctor said
oncology and his wife began to sob, some memory
of distraction, dandelions too high in the front lawn,
clipping the baby's fingernail too low, a cotton ball
pressed too tightly against a boil of blood that never
needed a Band-Aid. Make it a slow dance, close, the kind
without weeds, bright yellow, the opposite of putting off.

KENNY BARON SPECIALS

MARILYN KRIETE

At seventeen, new to Vancouver and desperate for money, I walked the seedy side and scored a job at the State Hotel, a disintegrating flophouse hunkered atop a fragrant French bakery. No paperwork was required. I was hired on the spot by virtue of having climbed the pee-stained stairs and asking about the 'Help Wanted' sign. If I could do that, I could chambermaid the innards of the sorry State Hotel.

The State was run by a trio of merry delusionals. Mr. McGillivray, a silver-haired senior with wispy business experience, had purchased the joint with a silent partner, confident that replacing the lobby's flickering fluorescents and warped linoleum would transform the relic into a profitable tourist inn. The renos were pending, awaiting fresh income. Meanwhile, he'd hired Will Padilla, a lanky young Mexican, to man the front desk. The two men, opposite in every way except their quixotic naivety, played front of house to a house of horrors.

Will, fresh from his parents' Acapulco resort, seemed not to notice his new clientele were not well-heeled tourists, but dealers, pimps, prostitutes, addicts, drifters, and pensioners. He was a sleepy-eyed amigo who sprawled all day across the counter, dreaming about the Canadian house he imagined buying and the patterns he'd use to 'paper-wall' it, and the beautiful Canadian girl he planned to find and marry. There was little action at the front desk during the day, and when he wasn't replacing lost keys, his mind swirled with visions of his hoped-for bourgeoisie.

Neither man ventured from the lobby to the guest rooms. Nor did Lottie, the wizened head housekeeper who, after thirty years in house, had earned the right to gossip with management when she wasn't chain-smoking in the laundry room, stuffing deplorable linens into old machines. The abused sheets and towels were delivered by her minions: Cindy and me. My fellow chambermaid, a gorgeous, eighteen-year-old Gidget — equally lost — had been hired the same week. Together we ran the top three floors like flirty den mothers, tag-teaming the rooms with Pine-Sol and trash bags, and befriending the residents. Every day was an education.

At least half the tenants were permanent guests, or at least as permanent as anchorless, shattered souls can be, and we soon found our favorites. First was Kenny Baron, a rakish fifty-seven-year-old who dressed by nine each morning in a white shirt, bow tie, and plaid vest, and henceforth invited us to share a "Kenny Baron Special": a tumblerful of cheap sherry and rotgut whiskey, mixed over his rusty sink. To be polite, we'd take a few gut-churning sips and then watch Kenny drink his, transforming him from a cheerful morning person to a sobbing wreck over his Life's Regret: the drinking that capsized his marriage, decades ago. Each time, he'd pull out a fading wartime photo and show us his lost bride, weeping as if she'd just walked out. Kenny's wretched performance never failed to stun me. I could see his how his entrenched narrative mired him in a rut he'd never escape, even if he wanted to. He'd found the perfect excuse to drink himself to death.

Several doors down, we'd visit Earl, a charismatic black pimp from Detroit, who beguiled us with gleaming white teeth, honeyed speech, and endless innuendo. When Earl got dressed — never till late afternoon — he wore broad felt hats and belted overcoats, straight out of Motown. He lounged till noon, and he'd host from under the covers, languorous as a cat. His ebony eyes wandered our bodies like feathers, making us melty and off balance. On Mondays, he'd mentally undress us to gauge if we'd gained a pound or two since the previous Friday. Once, after I'd spent another weekend smoking pot and baking, he called me 'Thunder Thighs', an epithet laden with double meaning. He liked fresh towels and white girls and making us burn. But Cindy and I had boyfriends, and weren't for sale. Still, I harbored a shameful crush, simultaneously imagining falling into bed with him and being appalled by my wicked imagination. Cindy and I never talked about Earl; the feelings he stirred were too intimate. We just kept going back, as if pulled by the moon.

By midafternoon, Alabama Dan would be waking up on the fourth floor, ready to invite Cindy and me for a smoke from his extensive drug stash. Dan was a drifter, a draft dodger, and a mediocre con artist. He wore a wide leather hat over his long, greasy pony tail, even in bed, and, unlike Earl, never requested fresh towels because he never bathed. We held our breath while Dan compulsively strummed his guitar to accompany his confusing anecdotes and antiestablishment rambling. He was hard to take on many levels — olfactorily, morally, aesthetically — but we felt sorry for him, having lost most of his brain to drugs and depravity. Like Kenny, he served as a cautionary tale: *Do drugs, but don't overdo them. Never reach the point where you're wearing hats to bed. And mind your hygiene if you hope to have friends*. Alabama Dan had none, and while we understood why, we nobly tried to fill the void in his rotten life. Plus, he always had a complimentary joint or pipe of hash to buy our company.

A tiny, bright-eyed pensioner named Mr. O'Leary was another favorite. Mr. O kept to himself; he'd lived in the State for years and did his own cleaning. Every Tuesday, we had a standing appointment in the lobby to exchange laundry. He wore an ancient three-piece suit and was always chipper, in spite of hard knocks. Years ago, Lottie told us, he'd been a firefighter, a husband, and a homeowner. But life had eroded everything except his government pension, barely enough to cover rent and subsist on hotplate soup and noodles. Still, he pursued dignity: rising early and following a tidy schedule of walking, shopping, and library sitting, keeping himself occupied. His room, when we passed by, never stank, and he seemed to inhabit a brighter, cleaner world than his drug-addled neighbors.

One Tuesday, Mr. O'Leary missed his laundry appointment, but we barely noticed. The next week, realizing no one had seen him come or go for days, Lottie sent me with a spare key to investigate. As soon as I cracked the door and inhaled, I knew what I would find. But I had no idea how thoroughly three pounds of brains could splatter a floor, three walls, and the faded bedspread of an army-tucked bed. Or how empty and freighted a room vacated by suicide can feel. His tidy quarters were otherwise immaculate. On his bedside table was a slim ledger book, itemizing every purchase he'd made in the past year. Crackers, tinned milk, bars of soap. No next of kin.

I looked and recoiled for twenty horrified seconds before bolting to the lobby. Mr. McGillivray called the police, and Cindy and I spent the rest of the day avoiding the fourth floor. This time, Mr. O'Leary's room was professionally cleaned by discreet workers who locked the door behind them. For a long time, maybe until the State met its own death, the room stayed locked.

Poor Mr. O'Leary: his exemplary, miserable life was over. But the violence of his death haunted me. Why a gun, why so gruesome an exit? I couldn't imagine his despair. And I couldn't fathom a death where there was no one left to mourn.

For six immersive months, the State Hotel was my second, vicarious life. Cindy and I were free agents, as long as we dealt with the vomit, needles, empties, and mystery-stained linens from the overnight guests — the ones we never saw — and didn't pester Lottie with questions. We bounced from floor to floor on our springy young legs (no elevators in the State), chortling over Will and Mr. McGillivray's shared lunacy and Lottie's tenured uselessness, and marveling at the perks of a job where getting high all day was not only free, but advisable. Indeed, we couldn't have coped with the State's putrefaction without cannabis and Kenny Baron Specials. On rough days, when the overnight guests left disturbing residuals and Mr. McGillivray sensed we needed a boost, he'd splurge on croissants and petits fours from the French bakery, bringing the exquisite aroma of butter, chocolate, and almonds to jostle with the putrid lobby air.

And when melt-in-your-mouth pastry wasn't enough, Cindy and I would fortify ourselves with a beer-and-tomato-juice lunch at the nearest pub before wobbling back to work at the strangest university in town.

First-Place Winner — **Nonfiction**

The first line of this story drew me right into the thick of the scene. Excellent job. As the reader, I knew exactly where I was, what it looked like, and could even imagine the smell. This type of writing sets the stage for the reader to sit back and enjoy the story as it unfolds.

The author here pulls no punches as a host of unique characters are introduced. Each one has distinct traits and a special spot in the story. To pull that off in such a limited word count is kudos to the writing style and choice of vocabulary. This story filled with life lessons and stoned undertones made me cringe, smile, and cheer all at once.

Great job. Congratulations.

— Faye Arcand

The Litany of Waking

Scott Fitzgerald Gray

She awoke to darkness and a grinding headache, her teeth buzzing and her hands tingling with the residual power of the flare that had dropped her. She knew no more than that, her thoughts reeling within a storm of shadow. She tried to touch her thumbs to each of her twitching fingers, judging whether any had gone missing. She found she couldn't quite remember how many she'd started with, though.

She ran through the litany of waking, remembering first her name. Sabela. That sounded right. She heard it in her Ma and Da's voices in her mind, and was pleased that she knew them as well. She recalled her age, twelve summers. That was important.

She tried to focus on place and action. Where she was, why she was there. And in doing so, she remembered suddenly the imperative of not moving a muscle where she lay sprawled on her back in the darkness. That was more important by far.

It was the familiar information that focused you, her parents had taught her. When power surged as fire and lightning through an open coupling, or along a conduit that had looked well grounded at first glance, it could kill you quick enough. Sabela had seen it happen. What was worse, though, was that same power scrambling mind and memory. So it was that her

Ma and Da had taught her the litany of waking, sharpening the instinct to reset the mind and put it through its paces in response to any unexplained darkness. Making sure everything was where it was supposed to be.

She squinted. In the half-light, she could see bundles of cable that thickened and twisted along dark walls, looping around and through each other like the contents of a butcher's offal bucket. She counted them and realized that her numbers had come back finally. She counted her fingers. Nine, just like she remembered.

Why have you come, ghost?

The voice came from everywhere and nowhere at once. Sabela felt her mind settle to an absolute silence, her body doing its own best to follow. The only sound was her blood beating steady in her head.

Ghost. I know you hear me.

The voice hung in the air as light as well as sound, like Sabela had seen once at a town-park concert her Ma and Da had taken her to when she was young. That had been great fountains of blue and red and white arcing through the sky, marking the boom and brass of the orchestra. By contrast, the noise-light of the voice was a single shade of pale gold, shimmering through the shadow of her sight like fireflies.

"Go away, voice," Sabela said.

Strong words, ghost, but this is my place you find yourself in. You cannot pass through these halls unnoticed and unseen.

When the voice spoke, its firefly light shifted and drifted through the space around Sabela's eyes. She saw the dark lines of cables and conduits more clearly. She saw condensers set in rows of six by two, hanging limp like sow's teats and dripping dead oil. She saw a straight tunnel up behind her, saw a twisting course leading down as she craned her head, feeling the tug of her hair where she'd plaited it down to keep it out of her way while she worked.

She still didn't know where she was, but she had her choice of escape routes. That was something.

"There's no such things as ghosts." Sabela heard an echo in her words as she recalled how Nicolau had said that exact thing to her. She blinked at the memory as it fell into place, feeling the headache rattle around a bit. She recalled the others as well, and was glad of it. Xabier and Cibran, Iago and Rocha and Illiam. Her fellow scrappers. Nicolau was their master, but him and his pig prod she would have been happy to forget.

"I've got work to do," Sabela added, but the voice and the shadows gave her no response.

It had been early when Nicolau woke them all, the sky a bruise of blue and gold above the ash fields. Sabela and the rest of the scrappers had been scouring those empty battlefields for the better part of the summer months. Long days spent in claiming old iron and bits of mechwork, lost among the smoldering fires that had burned since the end of the war.

It was meant to be a small war, the stories all said. The mechwork had changed that, though.

"The ruins is safe, you slack duff." Beneath the dark dawn, Nicolau had taken on the mocking tone he adopted in response to fear and injury among his scrappers. Sabela remembered him smirking through the time he'd cut and sealed the stump of her finger when it was lost. "The experts and the spook squads is gone through it six ways from the end times, and claimed it all clear."

"Then ask the experts and the spook squads what's there, and save me the trip."

Something in Sabela's thoughts seized up, so that she couldn't remember what Nicolau had said in response. She felt pretty certain the pig prod had been involved, though.

She remembered walking alone toward the ruins, the other seekers working the safer open ash behind her. This was a job for just her, Nicolau had said. He'd heard rumors of something big. Sabela picked her way along pathways of ash, watching for strike-spots of fire and lightning. Ahead was a great field of tangled steel strung with flapping canvas like wind-blown flags. Dangerous for a seeker not at the top of her game.

"There's no such things as ghosts," Nicolau had said. "There's just dead machines for halfwit folk to be afraid of. Not a proven tinker like you. You're not afraid, are you Sabi?"

Nicolau was the only one who called her Sabi. She hated it.

In the dark now, Sabela found her starling hanging from her belt. In response to her touch, it unfurled its wings and set itself into motion, mesh gears spinning up to a staccato clacking hiss. She set its lamp alight, fingers flicking control studs along its spheroid body, then tossed it to the air.

In the flying scutter's shimmering light, she saw the spark switch whose spasm of white lightning had coursed through her to put her down. The switch was a dead-drop condenser, set up to store all the power shunted into it when its circuit went dark. She should have gone back down the line, looked for a shunt point and grounded out any stray charge there. It was a novice seeker's mistake, its obviousness burning for a moment in Sabela's heart.

She was no plain seeker, though. She was a tinker, and the best in Nicolau's troupe. She was ready for this.

You are ready for what, ghost?

The words at her ear caught her by surprise. "You can go anytime, voice."

No. You are the one not meant to be here.

"Wrong about that."

The light of the starling showed Sabela where to go as she flexed and flicked an insulated prod from her belt kit into the switch. She had no need anymore to fear the white lightning she'd so effectively grounded out on herself. When that was done, she followed the starling along the spark lines, checking each connection where it split off from the main. She watched the scutter's lamp flash coded signals to mark each point of power detected as it went. She noted which points had worked loose and carefully tightened each in turn, knowing their power would be hungry for her fingers.

The starling was the newest of the countless types of scutter that Sabela shaped from mechwork scraps and tatters. The snake she pulled from her jacket pocket was one of her first pieces, simple in design but most effective. It coiled its oiled links around her wrist as its head lit up, giving her a working lamp as she checked and tightened a dozen wire fittings. When she was done, she punched the standby power active and held her breath.

With a bang, that power surged. She heard cables crackle, saw slack pipes pulse out with sudden pressure. A humming sounded out from the walls and floor as arc glow flared around her, and she shielded her eyes for the moment it took them to adjust.

When she looked out again, she had remembered where she was.

And where is that, ghost?

"*Behemot*," she whispered. "It's mine."

She had tripped across the name by accident, etched into the edge of a shattered wing. Most of the morning had already gone to routine salvage and avoiding the collapse of ash pits filled with rusting iron before she saw it. Her breather had howled against smoke and ash as she dug deeper to fully realize what she'd found, working her way in through layers of steel and rotting canvas. The remains of the last vessels *Behemot* had destroyed as the legendary airship fell to its doom.

Sabela remembered why she was there. She felt the last pieces of everything fitting into place in her head, locking in tight. "I'm going to make *Behemot* fly again. I'm going to show them all."

She realized she was answering a question no one had asked. She shrugged as she collected her tools, setting the starling to sleep at her belt again.

You should not be here, ghost.

"Got work to do, voice," she said. "Stay out of my way."

Sabela took the twisting passage leading down, away from the entrance she had carefully opened up through a blast port almost as wide as she was. She crawled slowly, checking for stray power coursing where it shouldn't. The interior of the engine core that she had cut her way into was remarkably intact, though. It spoke to the strength with which the great airship had been built, its interior struts and trusses as thick around as Sabela's waist.

Like a sinuous squirrel, she crawled through nests of cables that quivered with the standby power pulsing through them, ready to shunt fire and lightning to the sails and blast ports that had once taken *Behemot* to the air. In the darkest days of the Great War That Was, the airships that unleashed bright death from the sky had coursed like birds across a hundred nameless battlefields. But *Behemot* was the greatest of those airships, whose creation had swung the tide of war, and whose fall and destruction had ultimately lost it.

Except *Behemot* wasn't destroyed, and Sabela was the only person in the world who knew that.

What is it you seek, ghost?

"I'm going to make *Behemot* fly. You don't listen very well, voice."

I wasn't asking your orders. I was asking your goal.

"You know."

And how would I know?

"Because I'm imagining you." That realization settled in Sabela even as the words were spoken, and she felt the satisfaction that came of having solved that puzzle. "I got the pulse shock in me. Scrambled my thoughts, and you're what's left over."

It was a thing that happened sometimes. All scrappers lived with those risks as they scoured blackened battlefields in search of clean iron and precious brass. Insignias and medallions in gold and silver, sometimes, ready to fetch real coin in the pawnshops in the larger towns of the frontier. And above all else, the precious mechwork that had once turned the ash-grey battlefields red with blood and fire.

How do you know the pulse shock did not kill you? The tone of the voice was flat in her mind, but Sabela thought she felt it mocking her.

"Because if I was dead, I'd remember dying. You remember the things that happen to you."

By your logic, ghost, you were never born.

"I remember my Ma and Da. You lose, voice."

That was half a lie. She remembered her Da mostly, her Ma gone earlier to become just traces of voice and memory now. It was her Ma who had first showed her the tinker's ways, letting Sabela help repair the mechwork that her father collected, and that came in to their wagon for repairs when they traveled the trade roads.

With those tinker's ways, Sabela turned bits of still-functioning mechwork not large enough to sell to the machinists in town into the scutters that she and the other children used to search and sweep into tangled wreckage and unseen spaces. The dangers of those spaces gave most scutters a short life and highlighted their usefulness in keeping the scrappers from getting hurt, but Sabela was always happy to build new ones.

There were good seekers among Nicolau's troupe. Cibran and Illiam were the best, after her. No one else had Sabela's tinker's touch for the mechwork, though. That wasn't a thing you could teach, her Ma had always said.

The strength and precision with which *Behemot* had been built made the long day's job of restoring the engine core a simpler matter than Sabela would have thought. It was mostly time and rote labor, working her way one by one through power linkages torn free from their conduit lines. She patched and prodded. She repaired bright brass coils melted from the fatal heat of *Behemot*'s fall, hunting down free wire from the less important lighting systems to rewrap them. She bypassed and rerouted, listening always to the instinct of her touch and the readings the starling gave her as it flitted through the shadows.

When she was done, she rested a while. She took a drink of water from a skin bulb, tasted the grit of the ash fields that never seemed to wash away.

What are you, ghost? With your tools and your deft touch?

Sabela knew she was talking only to herself, but her pride made her answer. "Tinker. The best thing in Nicolau's troupe." As she shifted along a narrow gantry, she saw a filter pack below that marked the head of an airway. With the power systems patched, the airways would be her first approach to the controls that would test that power.

And what is Nicolau?

Sabela scowled as she remembered the pig prod. "He manages things. Buys and sells what we find for him."

Your captain, then.

"If you like." She pulled the filter pack free to peer into an air shaft beyond, battered but clear.

So when you resurrect the airship as you hope to do, it will be on Nicolau's order. He is the one who sent you here, tinker.

"Won't matter it's his order. I tell them I'm the one who patched *Behemot*, I'll prove I'm more than just a scrapper. I'll get out from under him. I'll find some place better."

Sabela hadn't really thought the words until she spoke them, but she felt them ring true. She had traveled with Nicolau since her father died because she had nowhere else to go. He kept her down, though. Wouldn't take her to the cities where she could do real work. Always just scrapping because that was what Nicolau knew.

We called you mechs before, the voice said, and Sabela thought she heard a strange wistfulness in its tone. *Tinkers. Working the machines and shaping their power for the captains to control.*

Sabela heard her Ma's voice in her mind suddenly. Not a thing she wanted to think about right now, needing to focus. "Talking to the mechwork isn't something to be taught..."

The floor beneath her feet gave way suddenly. A section of support lattice had been eaten away by lightning, the bars looking iron-solid but turning to black powder with a touch.

She was wary but not fast enough, swinging for an out-thrust support with both hands but only slowing herself as she fell.

She tumbled, hitting once. A long space of weightlessness told her the darkness she fell through was larger than she'd seen before. She hit a second time and stopped.

You should not have come here, ghost.

Sabela felt her heart skip an unexplained beat at the sudden sadness in the voice. She fumbled the snake from her belt and set its glow to full bright, then sent it crawling up high so that light would spread.

Black ash covered the wide expanse of windows above her, thick glass intact but showing fracture lines, rainbow bright. Sabela saw chairs and consoles canted sideways, to tell her the angle at which *Behemot* had settled beneath the ash. The confines of the engine core had come with no real sense of up and down, but she was reoriented now as she marked out the shadowed space of the great airship's flight deck.

Most of the crew who had died there were still in their chairs, dry rot stripping their flesh away, eating into canvas straps and dark grey uniform jackets. Their heads were slumped over and down in deference to gravity, but most of them still had their hats on. Other bodies were tumbled into heaps along the side of the deck, which was below Sabela in the orientation of the crash that had turned left to up, right to down.

Along all the walls, she saw the shadows move.

It wasn't a trick of the light, the snake coiled motionless above her. It wasn't a trick of her eyes. She worked the litany of waking again to clear her thoughts, but the words ground down beneath a rising fear as the darkness began to swirl around her. Watching her.

“What are they?” she whispered.

Ghosts, the voice said. *Like you.*

High above her, Sabela saw the deck’s power panel, no sign of damage to it. She frantically sent the starling up, flitting through the air on quick flaps of canvas wing to latch itself onto the panel’s key breaker. She read the power spooling there in the codes of the scutter’s flashing lamp.

“No such things as ghosts,” she whispered, trying to calm herself as the shadow flowed like liquid. She remembered words of her Ma’s as she backed away. “Spirit’s in the living body. Spirit’s the flow of blood and thought, and the dead have got no use of it.”

So the living say. The dead say it differently.

Sabela jumped for the vertical floor and climbed desperately, the shadow flowing to pursue her. She felt it reaching for her as she scrambled across cable and rough lattice, climbing over and past a body spilled out to hang free when its chair mount had snapped in two. At the height of the cantilevered deck, she slung herself onto the power panel, feeling it pulse beneath her. Ready for her.

There are ghosts in all machines, the voice said. *The special among the mechs can speak to them in their own way. Like you. Even if the ghosts seldom speak back.*

Her hands were a blur as she set the panel switches for start-up. The voice was shrill in her head, and with each word, she felt a faint spike in the power she aligned and activated.

These ghosts are screaming now, though, to tell you they are the spirits of this machine of war and they are tired of killing.

“They should have stopped me when I came in, then.” Sabela saw the panel lights go green beneath their cracked glass. She grabbed the key breaker with both hands.

We are tired of killing. Please, ghost.

She felt herself in the belly of a beast that generals had named for ancient legends and fearful portents. She remembered the stories from when she was a girl, the war not that long done but already more than ready to be turned to dark tales. She felt the fear of those tales now, of mechwork engines that had parted battlefields like steel plows through wet loam. Machines whose skin was cold iron and coursing fire. She knew the tales of the terrible tide of war *Behemot* had unleashed, and how the great airship had vanished in the end within a storm of elemental fire like the world had never seen.

She focused to push the visions away. "I don't care whatever war you were in."

We care about the next war, which begins when the monster you wish to resurrect screams its way to the sky once more.

"Folk won't fight again. That's what everyone says. Show them *Behemot* come back, and they'll be too scared to fight."

Other folk have said those same words. And sixteen millions died to prove them wrong, ghost.

"I'm not the ghost!" Sabela screamed it, fighting the fear.

You will be, child.

She meant to turn the key breaker. She was ready to feel the power surge that she had spent the long day reshaping. But she pulled the breaker instead, hauling on it with both hands to tear it free of its housing. As the growling hum of *Behemot* ground down to silence, she threw it helplessly at the shadow that swirled around her now.

"There's no such things as ghosts." Sabela's throat hurt.

No, child. If you were dead, you would remember dying. Or so you said. And so the dead do remember. We are the spirits of war, driving death before us. We are what's left when the power of the world is corrupted to destroy that world, leaving ash and madness in its wake.

"Let me go..."

Yes, child.

The shadow rose around and past her. Sabela saw it swirling around the starling. She felt something change.

To feel the flow of energy within mechwork is a thing that cannot be taught, the voice said. *Your mother told you true. It is a gift of fate that few share in, and which fewer still will ever master.*

"Let me go," Sabela said. She felt less afraid now.

Yes, child. We will go.

A blood-red sunset carried her back toward the camp one slow step at a time. She saw Nicolau watching for her, then pushing forward to close the distance as she drew near. Not too close, though. It was dangerous in the ash.

"Got everything I could." In the bag Sabela hefted over her shoulder, she had claimed a choice assortment of bulbs and wire, of mechwork bits salvaged from the shattered airships that had buried *Behemot*, before she walked away. It would fetch good coin, but was common enough that Nicolau would have no reason to go back in search of more.

"Nothing big?" he muttered. "I heard rumors."

"The experts and the spook squads called it clear. Listen to them next time."

Nicolau glared as he swung the pig prod, though with a sense of obligation more than malice.

"No," Sabela said.

She felt the power of the prod pulse to full life, its condenser drained in a heartbeat to arc past its insulated grip. Nicolau's lank hair shot out in a haze of grease and static lightning as he was knocked over backward with a scream.

The other scrappers drew closer. Sabela nodded to them all. She picked up the pig prod where it had fallen, watching as a trace of shadow detached from the snake coiled around her wrist and slipped inside it.

"Must be faulty," she said. "I'll fix it for you."

Nicolau growled as he stood, dusting himself off. "Don't be thinking above your place, Sabi."

"My name's Sabela."

She ran through the litany of waking as the others followed her back to the camp, Nicolau watching confused from the shadows behind them. Her name, her age.

Sabela, the ghost said to her ear. *Twelve summers.*

Place and action. Where she was, why she was there. She'd spend more time thinking about that, now that she had someone to talk to.

More **Precious**

Blu & Kelly Hopkins

When my hand held a pen I was a poet
when my hand touched the plow I worked the farm
when my hand found the sea I was a sailor
when my hand brushed the strings I was a bard

When your hand touched my face you were my lover
When your hand took my hand I found your soul
When you showed me your heart I learned of beauty
And your love is the gift that makes me whole

As through this wide world I wandered alone
searching for someone to hold
I never dreamed I would find such as you
more precious than diamonds or gold
more precious than diamonds or gold

We have stood side by side through storm and sorrow
and together have made our memories
as we sing of our love we are united
and our voices will rise in harmony

As through this wide world I wandered alone
searching for someone to hold
I never dreamed I would find such as you
more precious than diamonds or gold
more precious than diamonds or gold

Authors and Judges

Faye Arcand is an agented author under contract to The Rights Factory. Her first novel is a YA contemporary thriller. She is also an award-winning short story writer, freelancer, columnist, and blogger. She loves to travel the world to study people, cultures, and places. She is currently finishing up her second novel as well as a non-fiction book about the writing world and preparing a book proposal based on her popular newspaper column "Auntie Says." Her favorite things to do are to teach, encourage, and chat about writing. Faye lives in the South Okanagan with her family, ever-faithful dog, and sassy calico.

Faye was the nonfiction judge for the 2020 Askew's Word on the Lake Writing Contest.

Nancy Davies moved to Sooke after many years living in Vancouver and working at the Vancouver Public Library. In Sooke, she found a wonderful writing community centred around the Sooke Writers' Collective, which provides the support and inspiration often needed to write and take risks — like entering writing contests. She lives in a little house with her dog Ed, surrounded by trees, with a view of the ocean. Sitting in the carport is a restored 1974 turquoise VW bus named Clementine, who is just waiting for the all-clear to go on adventurous road trips. Nancy and Ed can't wait.

Scott Fitzgerald Gray (9th-level layabout, vindictive neutral) is a writer of fantasy and speculative fiction, a fiction editor, a story editor, and an editor and designer of roleplaying games — all of which means he finally has the job he really wanted when he was sixteen. He shares his life in the Canadian hinterland with a schoolteacher, two itinerant daughters, and a number of animal companions. More info on him and his work (some of it even occasionally truthful) can be found by reading between the lines at insaneangel.com.

Blu & Kelly Hopkins are an award-winning, songwriting, multi-instrumentalist duo. Focusing on original material, their extensive repertoire lets them blend traditional and contemporary tunes into their show with a dash of humour to achieve an entertaining, exciting, yet mellow brew of good times and good tunes. The couple have been travelling, writing songs and performing them for many years. Their writing draws from their shared experiences. They have lived the songs they sing. Blu & Kelly have presented numerous workshops in songwriting and performance, and teach guitar, banjo, mandolin, bass, and harmony singing in their Silver Creek recording studio. Their discography includes five recordings and they are currently working on their sixth CD project.

Richard Kelly Kemick is an award-winning poet, journalist, and fiction writer. His new nonfiction book, *I Am Herod*, takes readers backstage and undercover at one of the world's largest religious events. Having published widely in all three genres, Richard's work has been included in anthologies in Canada and the United Kingdom. He is the recipient of multiple awards, including two National Magazine Awards and a Writers' Guild of Alberta Award. He divides his time between Calgary, Alberta, and Rossland, British Columbia.

Marilyn Kriete now lives in Kelowna after a colorful life spanning four continents and sixteen cities, earning her keep as cook, chambermaid, waitress, fisherwoman, missionary, speaker/teacher, tutor, and academic writing editor. Her poetry and nonfiction have appeared in *The Lyric*, *Storyteller*, *The Eastern*

Iowa Review, and *Brevity Blog*. She has two completed memoirs, with a third on the way, and is actively seeking an agent/publisher. Her blog can be found at purplesplashofglory.com.

Sarah de Leeuw has a PhD in cultural-historical geography and a degree in creative writing, and is a professor who holds a Canada Research Chair in Humanities and Health Inequities with the Northern Medical Program at UNBC, the Faculty of Medicine at UBC. Her scholarly and creative work focuses on marginalized people and geographies, especially in Northern British Columbia. She is the author of the poetry collection *Outside, America* and the editor of three textbooks and six books of poetry and creative nonfiction, and her writing has received a Western Magazine Gold Award, two CBC Literary Awards, a Dorothey Livesay Award, and nominations for both the Rodrick Haig Brown Award and the Governor General's Literary Prize for nonfiction. In 2017, she was appointed to the Royal Society of Canada's College of New Scholars, Artists and Scientists.

Sharon McInnes is the author of *Across a Narrow Strait* (2018) and *Up Close & Personal: Confessions of a Backyard Birder* (2010). She has published articles in various magazines and newspapers. Her personal essay, "Formative Years," was included in *Writing the West Coast: Artful Identities* (Key Publishing House, 2012.) In June 2020, her short story "The David and Goliath" will be published in *Island Writer Magazine.* Sharon lives in Cumberland, where she is currently working on a book of personal essays, writing short stories, and enjoying being a grandma. She invites you to check out her website at sharonmcinnes.com.

Pamela Medland is a graduate of Simon Fraser University (BA) and the University of Toronto (MA, MLS). Her work has appeared online and in print in literary journals and anthologies in Canada and the United States, including *CV2*, *Freefall Magazine*, *Grain Magazine*, *The Prairie Journal*, *The Spadina Literary Review*, and others. Her first chapbook, *Bright Blade*, was published by Loft 112 in 2020. Pamela grew up on the west coast but now lives in Calgary. When not writing poetry, Pamela serves as director of the Airdrie Public Library.

Debbie Pakka has always written poems and fictional stories in her spare time. With an intense interest in psychology and relationships, her advice column "Dear Ellen" was syndicated in 1988 and ran for two years in a variety of BC newspapers. Encouraged by an editor from a Vancouver-based Woman's magazine who showed interest in her work, she began to write in earnest until life became busy with family and work. Recently retired, she now has time to "rekindle the flame." Debbie credits the Shuswap Writers' Group for inspiring her.

Océane Picard is a new Canadian resident, arriving from France. After falling in love with English, she decided to study the language and travel around the world to practice it. She found Enderby in 2015 and has been calling it home ever since. Océane started writing fan fiction and poetry during her teenage years, and recently started working on short stories and a novel project. She draws her inspiration from her travel and the colourful characters she's met along the way, always infusing her stories with a hint of magic.

David A. Poulsen has been a broadcaster, teacher, professional cowboy, football coach, stage and film actor and — most of all — writer. His writing career began in earnest when his story

"The Welcomin' " won the 1984 Alberta Culture Short Story Competition. Now the author of 27 books, the UBC Creative Writing alumnus and former Writer in Residence at the Saskatoon Public Library recently made his inaugural foray into the world of adult crime fiction with the best-selling Cullen and Cobb Mystery series. The fourth book in the series, *None So Deadly*, hit bookstores in May of 2019. David lives on a small ranch in Alberta's foothills southwest of Calgary.

David was the fiction judge for the 2020 Askew's Word on the Lake Writing Contest.

Sally Quon lives on the traditional and unceded territory of the Syilx people in the Okanagan Valley, and spends her time blogging her backcountry adventures and reading poetry to the cat. She has been published in *Chicken Soup for the Soul: The Forgiveness Fix*, and was long-listed for the Vallum Poetry Prize. Her bucket list is entirely about bears.

S. Maggie Ricciardi is a retired nurse, has lived in the Okanagan since 1984, and has attended almost all of the Word on the Lake Writers' Festivals. She comes from a family of writers who always encouraged her, and has written ever since she learned to read. She writes mostly short stories, articles for the *Okanagan Historical Society Report*, and articles in newspapers and magazines. She considers herself a relative newcomer to poetry writing, learning by reading our wonderful Canadian poets, and experimenting.

Linda Rogers is a former Victoria Poet Laureate and Canadian People's Poet, as well as a journalist, novelist and songwriter. The winner of numerous national and international awards and past President of the League of Canadian Poets and BC Federation of Writers, she has lectured at UBC and UVic and has a

Master's degree in Canlit. Linda collaborates in songwriting and children's books with her husband, mandolinist and illustrator Rick van Krugel. Most recent titles include: *Yo! Wik'sas? Hello! How Are You?*; *Crow Jazz*; *Bozuk*; and *The Empress Trilogy* from Ekstasis Books.

Linda was the poetry judge for the 2020 Askew's Word on the Lake Writing Contest.

Wendy Weseen was born in England and immigrated with her family to Saskatchewan in 1955. Though her family moved to Hope, British Columbia, Wendy stayed in Saskatchewan, married, and raised three children while working as an artist, community developer, and social worker. She obtained degrees in humanities, social work, and fine art, and was awarded the Most Distinguished Student Award for studio art and the Silver Medal in Fine Art from the University of Saskatchewan. Wendy has exhibited in numerous solo and group shows, incorporating diverse themes into her art that she carried into writing poetry and a newspaper column in *The Connector* in Kamloops. Recently, her work was accepted for a chapbook (a marriage of poetry and visual art).

The Shuswap Association of Writers celebrates the written word!

How do we do that? By:

- Connecting readers and writers with authors and their works
- Organizing the Word on the Lake Writers' Festival — a major literary event in the interior of British Columbia, which brings together writers, readers, published authors, editors, and publishers in an exciting and stimulating weekend festival.
- Promoting literacy in the Shuswap

SHUSWAP
association of
WRITERS

- Providing relevant workshops in our community related to all aspects of writing
- Promoting authors by arranging public readings
- Working with young writers through the Kidswrite Contest
- Organizing Young Writers workshops
- Providing opportunities for writers to showcase their work through the Askew's Word On The Lake Writing Contest and the Word on the Lake Anthology

Join the Shuswap Association of Writers today and receive registration discounts at SAW-sponsored events, advance notice of regional events, invites to local author book launches, and more!

Go to shuswapassociationofwriters.ca for information.

www.ingramcontent.com/pod-product-compliance
Lightning Source LLC
Chambersburg PA
CBHW021336060726
47591CB00006B/2050

* 9 7 8 1 7 7 7 1 9 9 3 0 2 *